design with
paper

IN ART AND GRAPHIC DESIGN

This handsome paper-sculpted eagle is the much-used symbol of the Simpson Paper Company of San Francisco, California. The photograph is by Abrogast of Palo Alto. The eagle is used in many ways, including embossing on printed material by Simpson. The designer of the original sculpture was Steve Jacobs, who was assisted by artist Norman Orr.

design with
paper

IN ART AND GRAPHIC DESIGN

RAYMOND A. BALLINGER

 VAN NOSTRAND REINHOLD COMPANY

NEW YORK   CINCINNATI   TORONTO   LONDON   MELBOURNE

To a large number of former students who
survived my demanding criticisms and have
gone on to be distinguished artists and
graphic designers—and my friends.

Copyright © 1982 by Van Nostrand Reinhold Company Inc.

Library of Congress Catalog Card Number 82-1853

ISBN 0-442-24491-6

Printed in the United States of America

Published by Van Nostrand Reinhold Company Inc.
135 West 50th Street
New York, New York 10020

Van Nostrand Reinhold Publishing
1410 Birchmount Road
Scarborough, Ontario MIP 2E7, Canada

Van Nostrand Reinhold Australia Pty. Ltd.
17 Queen Street
Mitcham, Victoria 3132, Australia

Van Nostrand Reinhold Company Limited
Molly Millars Lane
Wokingham, Berkshire, England

16 15 14 13 12 11 10 9 8 7 6 5 4 3 2 1

Library of Congress Cataloging in Publication Data

Ballinger, Raymond A., 1907–
    Design with paper in art and graphic design.

    Bibliography: p.
    Includes index.
    1. Paper work.   2. Graphic arts.   I. Title.
TT870.B23   702'.8   82–1853
ISBN 0–442–24491–6   AACR2

CONTENTS

About Paper	6	**Packaging for Things and Thoughts**	72
About the Book	7	**Geometric and Abstract Forms**	90
Traditions in Paperwork	10	**Do-It-Yourself**	107
Die-Cutting and Folding	18	**Variations in Paper**	113
Embossing Paper	28	**Glossary**	140
Paper in Art Forms	40	**Bibliography**	142
Paper in the Graphic Arts	62	**Index**	

ACKNOWLEDGMENTS

In this book, as in others, I have been encouraged and supported by a host of people, most of whom cannot be acknowledged here. Throughout the book I have tried to include credits and permissions accurately.

First and always must be appreciation to my wife, Louise Bowen Ballinger, for her constant encouragement, criticism, and suggestions. Thomas J. Laverty entered the spirit of the project and contributed his expertise to photographic assignments. The following individuals have been unusually interested and helpful during the period of assembling material for the book: Edna Andrade, John William Brown, Xenio Cage, Jeanne Coombs, Bill Crawford, Ronald Dove, Richard DePaul, Harold Guida, T. Richard Hood, Judith Ingram, John Kroll, Jule Lambeck, Evelyn Pennegar, Fred deP. Rothermel, Ernest Schaefer, Ingebord Schulz, Marjorie K. Sieger, Barbara Torode, and Arthur P. Williams. Each of these people is distinguished in education, letters, or the arts.

ABOUT PAPER

Old rags, tree bark, hemp, fish nets, grasses, silk, vegetable fibers, flax, cotton, linen, starch, and animal glue are used to make *paper,* one of our most important commodities.

The process evolved about 2,000 years ago, and credit is given to Ts'ai Lun, a Chinese court official, for the invention of paper in 105 A.D. He was commended by Emperor Ho-ti, thus becoming known in China as the patron saint of papermaking. Before this time, many craftsmen had been searching for a material to take the place of the papyrus and silk commonly used for calligraphy. Silk paper is known to have existed, but there is no silk in Ts'ai Lun's paper; he used old rags, hemp, tree bark, and fish nets.

Today there is a great revival of interest in papermaking and many artists and craftsmen are busily engaged in a return to the making of paper by hand, creating art forms of unusual interest and merit. Some of their accomplishments are shown in this book. On the other hand, papers made by machine, using mechanical methods that are surprisingly similar to those used for hand-worked operations, are so numerous and commonplace that the average person takes paper for granted as a material for the daily news, for wrapping, containing, or carrying almost anything, for household uses, and for printing purposes. The artist, designer, and craftsman, however, do not take paper for granted; to them it is a challenging material, and they are very conscious and knowledgeable about its characteristics and qualities. Soft or hard, thick or thin, rough or smooth—these and other equally important factors must be carefully studied in relation to specific projects or assignments.

Paper has many extended uses that its inventors never foresaw. Ts'ai Lun certainly was not interested in cutting, folding, embossing or constructing. Yet in later times the Chinese and the Japanese contributed to the artistry of cutting paper for decorative, symbolic, and utilitarian uses. Untutored folk or tribal artists also created beautiful things by cutting or forming paper: items for tribal or ceremonial purposes, decorative pieces done for sentimental reasons, or stencils to be used for the embellishment of walls and boxes, to name a few.

Art and design students soon become aware of the difference in papers. The paper used for drawing purposes is usually not one that would be suitable for producing a watercolor. Nor would either of these be appropriate for lettering or instrumental drawing. One soon becomes aware of the differences between hot- and cold-pressed surfaces in bristol and illustration boards. At the very beginning of any project one's interests and knowledge of paper play an important part in the consideration and selection of the paper to be used, whether it be to work upon, to design with, or to print upon.

Soft, open-textured, handmade paper, which is suitable for enhancing the printing quality of an art subject, is unsuitable for the die-cutting of a folder or for the cover of a booklet or report, where a harder cover paper (paper manufacturer's term) is desirable. A strong bristol board (really not a "board" but a heavier weight of paper constructed in "plies" and purchased that way) is a good choice for constructions in paper. On the other hand, the paper chosen by the designer for experimentation must be reconsidered when the requirements of quantity production are involved.

When designing and working with paper one is inclined to think "white." But manufacturers are producing many papers in stunning color, sometimes vivid and sometimes soft, sometimes dull or textured, and sometimes glossy. These marvels of papermaking science extend the horizons of design with paper.

ABOUT THE BOOK

The examples shown in this book are limited to what has been *made* of paper. Though many items have printed matter on them, that is of secondary consideration. The manner in which a piece has been cut, folded, formed, or constructed of paper is the primary reason for its inclusion here. The aesthetic qualities of each piece are of utmost importance, although a few are shown because of their unexpected or novel use of the medium.

The book is organized into sections that illustrate the particular manner in which designers or artists have created with paper. It has not been planned as a "how-to-do-it" treatise; however, where it has been thought to be helpful, attention has been given to technical detail.

Items of antiquity as well as contemporary pieces which often use the same techniques are included. There are, for instance, old examples of fine embossing as well as contemporary ones.

The last part of the book includes some experimental pieces, never actually used, and another section includes miscellaneous items that did not seem to fit any previous category but show a variety of imagination and ingenuity in uses of this versatile material.

Carefully preserved objects and forms made of paper, found in private collections and in museums, give us a picture of their creators' activities and modes of living. Beautifully designed contemporary items, many of them mass-produced, evoke an enthusiastic response for one of our most common materials—paper. May the contents of this book be a challenge and a stimulus, particularly for young designers and artists who may contribute the results of their talents in the future.

The Chinese invented paper primarily for calligraphy, but it is not surprising that they gradually found ways to use it for other purposes, including papercutting. For a long time paper was either rare or expensive and these factors prohibited its use for pure decoration; also, paper was often reused, thus beclouding the records. Nevertheless, papercutting in China has a long history. By the seventh or eighth centuries there is evidence of the use of colored paper and papercut decorations.

The uses of papercuts have been many and varied. They were used as decorations for windows (themselves sometimes paper), walls, ceilings, and lanterns, and as stencils for lacquerware, pottery, and porcelain. They were also used as decorations for packages, temple offerings, gifts, fans, folding screens, and other objects, and as patterns for embroidery. The piece directly above is from *Chinese Cut Paper Designs* by Theodore Menten (Dover Publications, Inc., New York). The others are from the collection of Jeanne Coombs of Cherry Hill, New Jersey.

8

9

TRADITIONS IN PAPERWORK

The Chinese are credited with the invention of paper and have continued the art of papercutting even into contemporary times. It is the Japanese, noted for their great finger-dexterity and imaginative design concepts, who are renowned for the cutting of paper stencils for printing on fabrics and other materials. Japanese stencilcutting came into existence, it is believed, near the

end of the seventeenth century and flourished because the printing of fabrics for kimono-like garments created a great demand. The origin of the stencil above is of handmade paper made from two-ply mulberry bark fiber and is quite thin. The impressions from the stencil are made by placing it next to the surface to be decorated and brushing the pigment through the stencil with a brush made of human hair. This stencil is from the collection of Marjorie K. Sieger.

12

The papercuttings shown here are from Mexico. The figures on the facing page are magical barkpaper cutouts done by the Otomi Indians, who live in the Central Plateau of Mexico. The Otomi believe that the sun, earth, water, seeds, and air are beneficent deities to be honored with ceremonies; malevolent gods must be appeased in other rites. The dolls are cut from handmade mulberry and wild fig tree bark paper. Small, six-inch paper figures are cut out by healers or sorcerers and used in ceremonies. Dark paper represents evil spirits and white paper represents beneficent spirits. Evil spirits have pointed boots while the good spirits have bare feet.

The large Otomi figure shown at the top of the facing page is from the collection of Fred deP. Rothermel of Reading, Pennsylvania. I prepared the smaller silhouettes from authentic sources.

The example above is a contemporary decoration cut from tissue-thin colored paper, and there are many subjects cut from different colored papers as well as from white. It is about twice the size of this reproduction ($18\frac{3}{4}'' \times 28\frac{1}{2}''$). The original cutting is from the collection of Arthur P. Williams of Philadelphia.

13

While papercutting has been indigenous to artists of Oriental countries, paper valentines have been traditional in Europe and America for a long time. These have been in forms that are stamped, embossed, stand-up, folded with pure white paper or with papers in bright colors, and often aglow with paper ribbons and flowers. The valentines shown here are traditional forms but 14 their actual dates, unfortunately, are unknown. The richly elegant effect of lace in pure white paper (above) is shown on a valentine from the personal collection of Arthur P. Williams. The valentine at the bottom of the facing page is shown courtesy of the Henry Francis du Pont Winterthur Museum Libraries, Winterthur, Delaware, as is the unusual "lift-up" valentine shown at the top.

Paper cutouts for various purposes have long been a tradition in paper usage; the items shown here are American museum pieces. The handsome cut figures at the top of the facing page were in all probability used as toys for children. Note that one arm on each piece is on a simple swivel, which allows the arm and hat to be lifted in salute. These cutouts are shown courtesy of Henry Francis du Pont Winterthur Museum, Joseph Downs Manuscript Collection, Waldron Collection, Winterthur, Delaware.

The charming silhouette (left), which dates back to c. 1840, is a self-portrait by Wilhelm Muller (1804–1865) of Dusseldorf, Germany. The shadow puppets (above) for "Don Quichotte et la Moulin" were made from cut white cardboard in Paris, France, c. 1800. They are part of a series made for Theatre Seraphin. The Muller silhouette and the shadow puppets are reproduced courtesy of the Cooper-Hewitt Museum of Design, Smithsonian Institution, New York.

DIE-CUTTING AND FOLDING

Cutting holes and folding are two of the most fundamental techniques applied to paper other than printing itself. Die-cutting is a mechanical method for cutting paper, cardboard, or other material in regular or irregular sizes and shapes. A simple example would be a round hole cut in the cover of a booklet in order to allow text or pictorial material that appears on the inside page to be seen. Or the edge of a piece might be cut as desired by the designer—in the shape of a leaf, for instance. Hollow die and steel-rule die are the two methods of die-cutting.

Similar to a cookie cutter, the sharp-edged hollow-steel die is formed into a designed shape and set into metal or wood, which in turn is mounted on a heavy die press. Pressure of the press forces the die to cut through the thickness of the paper or other material.

A steel-rule die is used for cutting larger sheets and for accuracy. A form, usually the size of the printed sheet, is made up for the individual units to be cut. This form is then locked onto the bed of a printing or die-cutting press, positioned, and made ready. The sheets are cut one at a time in the case of a printing press; on a die-cutting press several sheets may be cut at the same time.

To achieve any die-cut piece the artist or designer first prepares line drawings of exactly the size and contours required. This may be a very simple form such as mentioned above or it may be a relatively complex design or even several forms to be cut in the same piece.

Folding is a common procedure in the printing industry and most folds can be made by folding machines, particularly if the designer has conferred with the printers about the requirements of the piece.

Simple elegance is expressed in these examples of die-cutting and folding for greeting cards. The triangular tree form (left) was sent by *TV Guide* of Radnor, Pennsylvania. The art director was John Brown and the designer, Dolores Alta-mura. "Cathedral" (below) by Ted Naos is shown with permission of The Museum of Modern Art, New York.

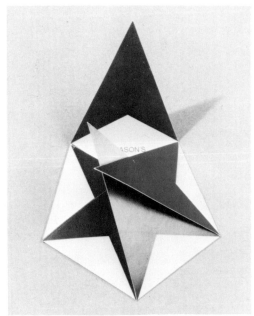

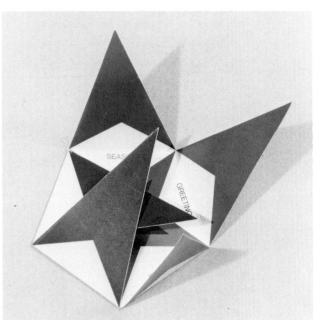

Two examples of die-cut and folded uses of paper are shown here. The "star" form, used for a holiday greeting card, is by *TV Guide* of Radnor, Pennsylvania. It was designed by Dolores Altamura and the art director was John Brown. The stylized "thumbs" portfolio was used to show the abilities of the Bruno Mease design group of Philadelphia. It enclosed miniature reproductions of examples of their design work.

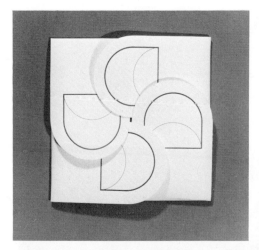
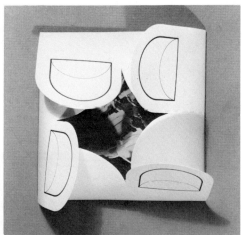

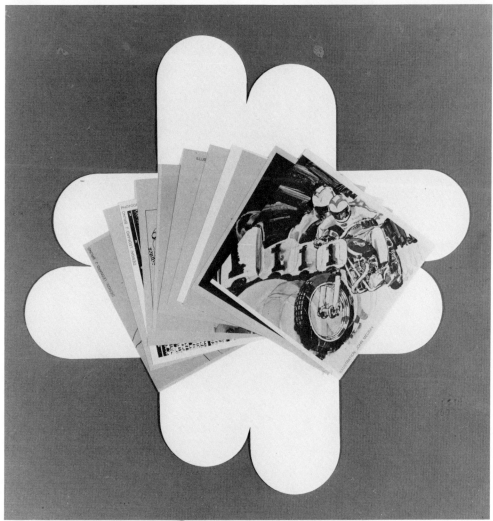

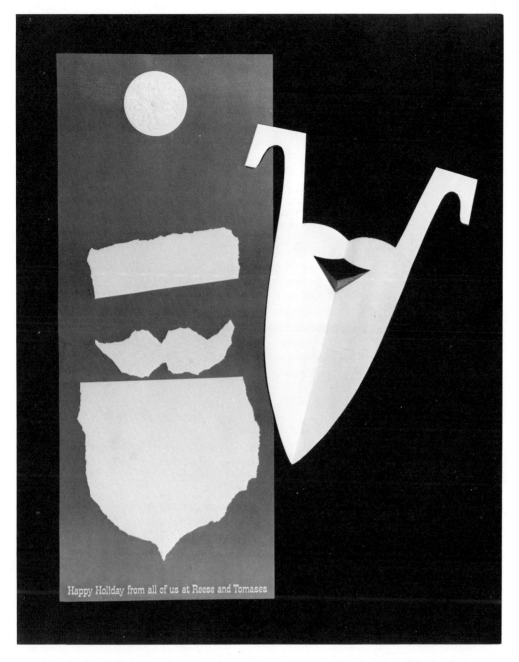

Happy Holiday from all of us at Reese and Tomases

Many of us remember the joy we experienced as children when we were shown that folded paper and a pair of scissors would produce accordion-folded figures or intricate Christmas snowflakes. Accordion folds and die-cuts are often employed in the graphic arts. The straightforward example at the top of the facing page was used as a direct-mail piece by *TV Guide* magazine; the art director was John Brown and the designer, Bobbi Adair. When expanded the piece is $31\frac{7}{8}''$ wide and 8" high. The holiday greeting card (middle) with five Santas in a row was designed and sent by Reese, Tomases & Ellick, Inc. of Wilmington, Delaware; it opens out to 25" and is $7\frac{1}{4}''$ high. Holidays and celebrations challenge designers to produce the unusual. The five jolly Santa Claus faces in the card at the bottom, with accordion folds and die-cut lips, was designed by Kramer, Miller, Lomden, Glassman of Philadelphia; this piece opens out to $13\frac{3}{4}''$ and is $8\frac{3}{4}''$ high. From the same design group is a die-cut beard (above) which recipients can hang over their ears; the beard measures 15" in depth. Torn paper and an embossed circle, also shown above, define the Santa Claus in the greeting card designed by Reese, Tomases & Ellick, Inc.; Santa's hat and beard measure $10\frac{3}{8}'' \times 24\frac{3}{4}''$.

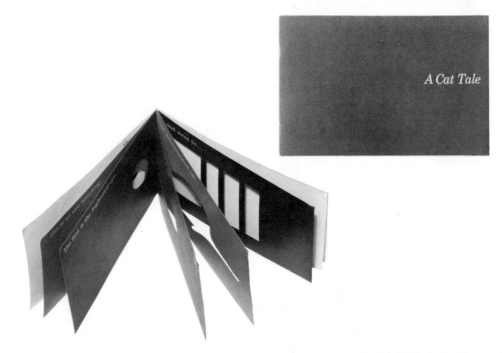

I can still vividly recall a children's book in which a hole through every page represented the path of a bullet fired accidentally by a careless youth. The little book shown here, *A Cat Tale,* is of a similar nature in that a mouse and the eye of a cat follow the die-cuts through the pages. The book was used by Upjohn Company of Kalamazoo, Michigan as an advertising piece for veterinary products and is shown here with their permission. It measures 8½″ wide by 5½″ high and is printed in several rich, flat colors.

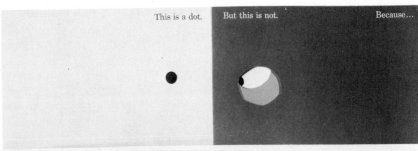

This is a dot.   But this is not.   Because...

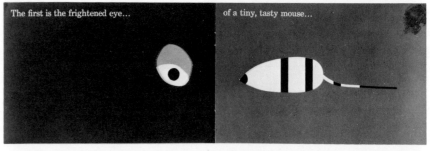

The first is the frightened eye...   of a tiny, tasty mouse...

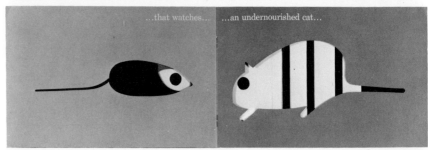

...that watches...   ...an undernourished cat...

...that swallowed the tasty mouse...   ...and went to...

24

The head of an osprey is die-cut and swings forward from the cover of this mailing piece for the Weyerhaeuser Company of Plymouth Meeting, Pennsylvania; it was designed by Elmer Pizzi, art director of Gray & Rogers, Inc. of Philadelphia. The osprey was photographed by David Hamilton. In addition to being die-cut, the osprey gains more realism by being subtly embossed. The cover is $8\frac{1}{2}'' \times 11''$, with the die-cut of the osprey measuring $7''$. This is a fine example of a die-cut used on the edge of a sheet rather than on the interior.

This huge, entertaining piece was designed for direct-mail usage for the *Saturday Evening Post* by the design team of Bruno Mease of Philadelphia. It embodies folds, a huge die-cut, and a pop-up and measures 43½″ when fully opened.

EMBOSSING PAPER

Embossing is a method that raises an image, letters, or a logo on blank material, such as paper, by dies of similar pattern, one a negative of the other. It is not a new technique—there are many examples of fine embossing produced during the 1800s. It is, however, a technique often used by artists, designers, and printers when an unusual or distinctive effect is desired. To the eye of the beholder, embossing often says "elegance."

The preparation of an embossing begins with original material, often in the form of line art, illustrations, photographs, or portraits. The engraver of the embossing plates renders these subjects in metal, often by hand. If the embossing is simple, the basic plate may be made by a photomechanical plate-making process. If it is an embossing of an elaborate item, such as a scenic subject, the plate is created with much hand work and can be costly. An embossed piece produced from a photographic subject is a hand process rather than a photomechanical one. The embossing or "molding" is accomplished by pressing the material (paper in this case) between the plates—a female die and a male bed or counter—both of which have been mounted to register in a press.

The whole process of making an embossing is a technical one and artists or designers need not be involved beyond the point of supplying the required art or design. It would be helpful, however, to observe embossing techniques firsthand. Embossings can be made—for various reasons—in different depths and the artist or designer should confer with the producer as to which would be advisable for their purposes. A cold press without heat may be used for light embossing and an electrically heated press for deeper embossing and fine detail. Gold, silver, or colored stamping-foil may be fed over the die when embossing by heat, thus leaving these pigments on the embossed area. This is called stamping.

An embossing plate for the National Quality Award of the Fidelity Mutual Life Insurance Company is shown at the top of the facing page; next to it is a simple embossed Q. At the bottom of the page is the cover for a paper-sample booklet for Carrara/Graphic Weave, which is manufactured by the Georgia-Pacific Corporation; it is handsomely embossed with the sculptured head of Michelangelo's "David," which was rendered from an excellent photograph of the subject. These pieces illustrate the different effects possible in embossing—from the elegant simplicity of a single letter to the intricate sculptured quality of the head.

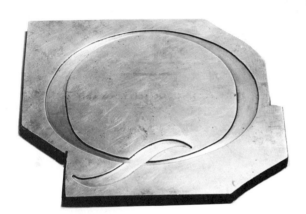

GILBERT A. HAGGART, C.L.U.

HAS BEEN GRANTED THE

1980

NATIONAL QUALITY AWARD

FOR THE FIFTEENTH CONSECUTIVE YEAR.

THE FIDELITY MUTUAL LIFE
INSURANCE COMPANY

This citation is awarded annually to
qualifying underwriters in recognition of
superior life insurance service to the public. The award
is presented jointly by the National Association of Life
Underwriters and the Life Insurance Agency Management Association.

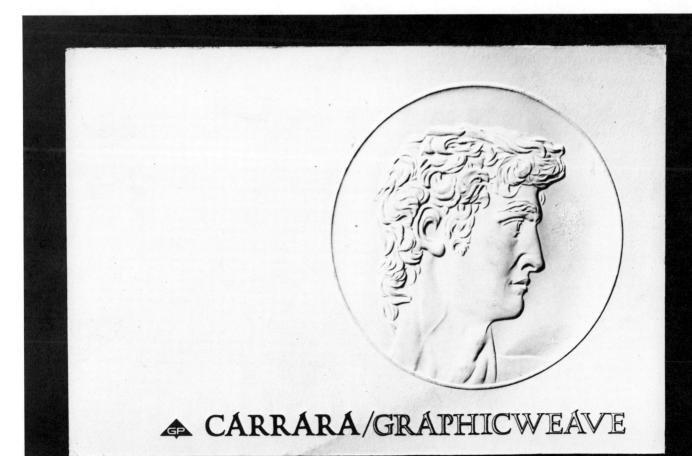

GP CARRARA/GRAPHICWEAVE

Stonelake

EMBOSSING DIE BY DANIELS ENGRAVING

EMBOSSING BY GOLDEN STATE EMBOSSING

The embossing dies of Daniels Engraving, Glendale, California,
are well-known and of excellent quality. The piece (facing page,
top) was embossed by Golden State. Rough or textured
paper is often used in order to enhance the quality of the
embossed areas. This effect is evident in the Stonelake embossing.

Victorian in its elegance, this admission card (above) informs of the presence of Queen
Victoria on Lord Mayor's Day in London in 1837. At the bottom
of the facing page is a contemporary example of very decorative embossing.
It is one of several Christmas greeting cards I have received year after year from Irving
Zucker of New York and is reproduced here with his permission.
The artist was the distinguished Andrew Szoeke, also of New York. All
of these pieces are reproduced somewhat smaller than the originals.

"Silent Crystal", 1972

The Simpson Paper Company of San Francisco, California, issues publications such as *Dimensions 44*. On the cover (left) is a paper sculpture eagle (see also page 2) used as an embossing on pure white paper. The original paper sculpture is by Steven Jacobs, assisted by Norman Orr. The embossing die for this cover was made by William A. Hammer of George R. Gehring Company, San Francisco.

The cover of a brochure (below) by the Hammermill Paper Company of Erie, Pennsylvania, shows an embossing of an entirely different nature. This, too, is on pure white paper and the freely designed "ghost" contrasts interestingly with the simple, mechanical letter forms. The design of this entertaining piece is by Thomas Lowes.

Many embossings are on pure white paper and their edges or contours are often crisp and tight. This is not true of the surprisingly different embossing (facing page) that was designed by Reese, Tomases & Ellick, Inc. for Sears Roebuck Acceptance Corporation, both of Wilmington, Delaware. A message attached to this holiday greeting states that "Silent Crystal is a specially commissioned embossed print [that] discloses the transient, unapparent design structure that is embodied in each crystalline snowflake that falls without a word."

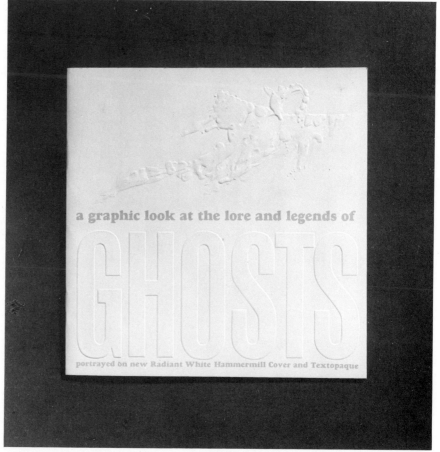

Commencement
Northeastern University
Boston Garden
June 22, 1975

General usage has left the impression that embossings are always on white paper, but this is not always the case. Both of the embossings of this page were done on rich, dark papers. The cover for the commencement booklet of Northeastern University in Boston (left) shows handsomely drawn leaf forms embossed on a rich red, textured Beckett Felt Cover paper by The Beckett Paper Company of Hamilton, Ohio. The cover was designed by Nancy Condry and printed by Clark-Franklin-Kingston Press.

The "spelunkers" cover (below) is on a wonderful booklet about underground exploration produced by Kimberley-Clark of Neenah, Wisconsin. The embossing is on their Dorset Brown Classic Text. The creative direction of the piece was by Klau-Van Pieterson-Dunlap, Inc. The art director was Bill Cook and design execution was by Advertising Art Studios, Inc. The embossing dies were made by Papercraft, Inc. and the platemaker and printer was Moebus Printing Company.

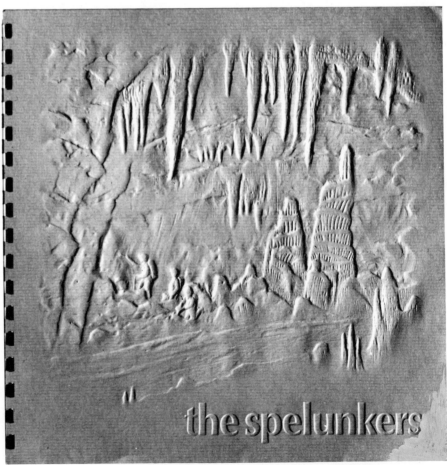

the spelunkers

The embossing on this page was apparently
accomplished on a very rough paper or board. It is from
a title page illustration in *Graphic Art of a Swiss
Town* published by ABC Verlag, Zurich, Switzerland.
It is the symbol of the municipal authority of
Zurich and was designed by Pierre Gauchat.

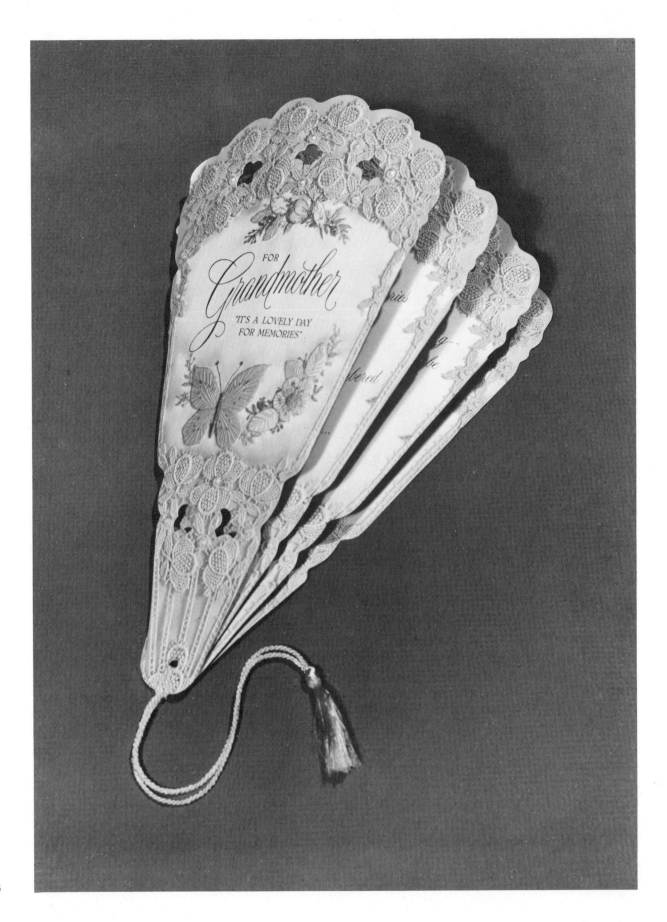

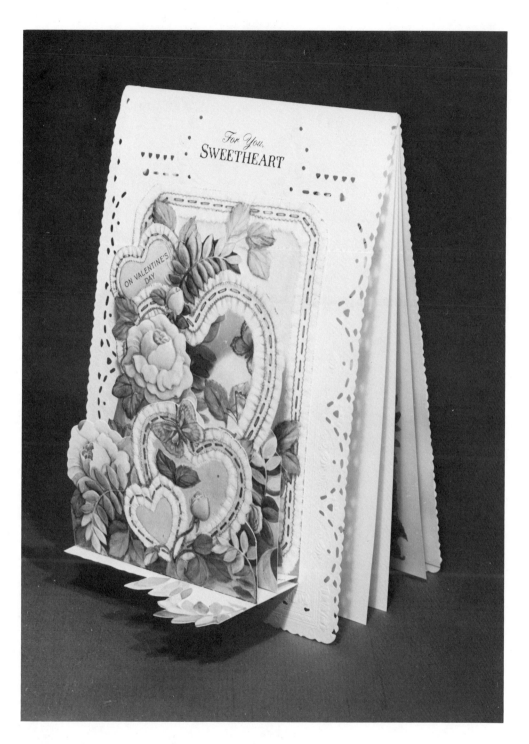

Embossing is often used to simulate other effects, such as lace-like texture, or to enhance floral forms. In addition to embossing, the greeting card for "Grandmother" (facing page) embodies many techniques that can be applied to paper including die-cutting, hinging, and full-color printing. These techniques are also applied to the stand-up "Sweetheart" card (above) in which the hearts and flowers fold out on a sort of three-dimensional shelf. Both pieces are shown courtesy of Hallmark Cards, Inc., Kansas City, Missouri.

These pages present a fitting climax to the preceding pages on die-cutting and folding and on embossing paper because these techniques, in addition to fine printing, have been used to advantage in making this stunning sample piece for Eagle A Velvetsheen paper, a product of Linweave, Inc. of

Holyoke, Massachusetts. The piece is 11″ high and when fully opened it measures 35¼″ in width. The design and production was by Designers 3 of New York City and the printing by Manhardt-Alexander of Buffalo, New York.

PAPER IN ART FORMS

A sheet of pure white paper is a thing of beauty and a challenge to the artist and designer. This has been so ever since its invention in China. Using paper first to write and paint upon—it was cheaper to produce than silk—the Chinese in later times began to cut paper art forms with great facility. Since then artists and craftsmen have often used paper as a medium for expressing ideas in art and design. Most of the art forms in this section have been executed with available papers that were readily adapted to their purpose. On the other hand, the making of paper by hand has had a revival of interest and action in the past few years. There have been numerous exhibitions in museums and galleries concerning art in paper, much of it handmade and very handsome.

The paper sculpture of George Washington is typical of the work of artist-educator Vincent Farralli of Philadelphia, Pennsylvania. The reproduction shown here is about one-third the size of the actual piece.

42

Examples of paper techniques found in museum and private collections seem to indicate that, without the diversion of radio and television, some of our ancestors turned to experimentation with paper to entertain themselves. At the top of the facing page is the interesting technique of pinpricking the back of a piece of paper in order to raise up a pictorial image. This charming piece is shown courtesy of the Henry Francis du Pont Winterthur Museum Libraries, Winterthur, Delaware. From the same collection; the intricate piece below is classified as a cutwork picture and dates 1800–1850. It is 9½″ wide by 7⅜″ high, while the other two pieces shown on these pages are approximately the same size as the originals. At the bottom of the facing page is an unusual little card (c. 1891) from the collection of Bill Crawford. In this case the design has been cut or sliced by a sharp instrument and lifted so that it creates almost the same effect as an embossed piece.

For a long time artists from many countries have involved themselves in papercutting or scissor cutting for purely decorative purposes. The Pennsylvania Germans call it *Scherenschnitte,* the French, *papier découpe.* The two examples shown here may be classified as cutwork pictures and each was done in the United States at a different period. The framed cutwork picture on this page is dated 1840 and measures 8⅝″ wide × 10⅝″ high. It is in the collections of The Henry Francis du Pont Winterthur Museum, Winterthur, Delaware. As can be seen in the illustration, the frame is filled with intricately cut paper flowers in a quaint arrangement. The example of papercutting (facing page) by Fred deP. Rothermel of Reading, Pennsylvania contrasts sharply with the examples of his work shown on other pages of this book. It is interesting to note that in this design there seems to be a symmetrical balance (as often appears in papercutting work), but further inspection shows that the elements on either side differ and this asymmetry makes it all the more intriguing. This elaborate piece is owned by Mrs. George Brooke III of Reading, Pennsylvania.

44

This elaborate expression of a queen's costume (above) is by artist-instructor Bill Crawford of Northfield, New Jersey, whose enthusiasm for paper as a medium of design is seen in other examples of his work in this book. The bold and rugged paper sculpture (facing page) for a cover of Weyerhaeuser Company's *Innovations In Paper* was done by James M. Reynolds and the model was Ivan Chermayeff, New York's distinguished designer, author, illustrator, and instructor. In addition to the modeling effect achieved by strips of paper—unusual in itself—the cover was also embossed by Fischer-Partelow, Inc., New York, on Weyerhaeuser Carousel cover stock.

INNOVATIONS
IN PAPER

Volume I, Number 2

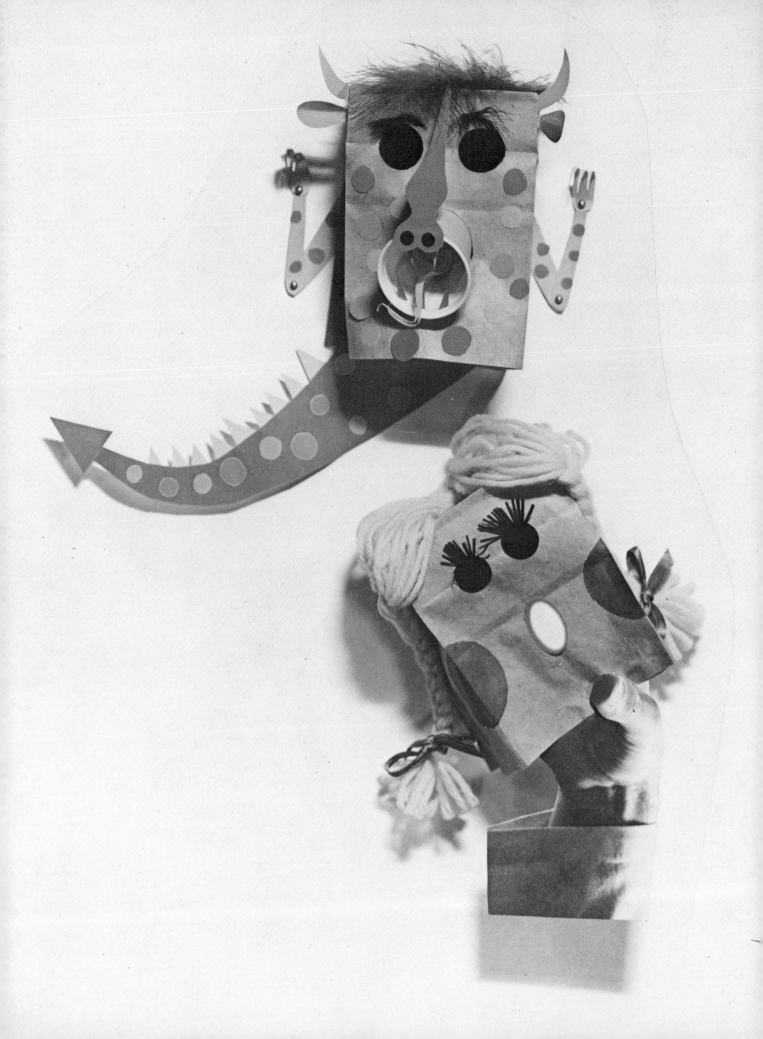

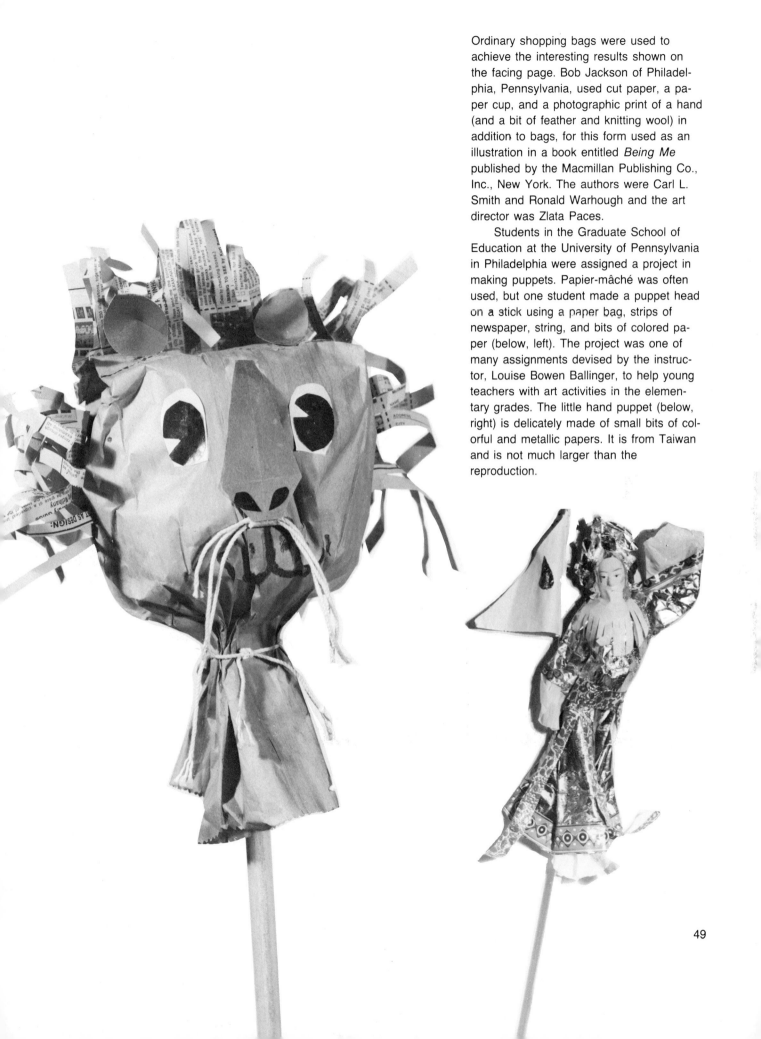

Ordinary shopping bags were used to achieve the interesting results shown on the facing page. Bob Jackson of Philadelphia, Pennsylvania, used cut paper, a paper cup, and a photographic print of a hand (and a bit of feather and knitting wool) in addition to bags, for this form used as an illustration in a book entitled *Being Me* published by the Macmillan Publishing Co., Inc., New York. The authors were Carl L. Smith and Ronald Warhough and the art director was Zlata Paces.

Students in the Graduate School of Education at the University of Pennsylvania in Philadelphia were assigned a project in making puppets. Papier-mâché was often used, but one student made a puppet head on a stick using a paper bag, strips of newspaper, string, and bits of colored paper (below, left). The project was one of many assignments devised by the instructor, Louise Bowen Ballinger, to help young teachers with art activities in the elementary grades. The little hand puppet (below, right) is delicately made of small bits of colorful and metallic papers. It is from Taiwan and is not much larger than the reproduction.

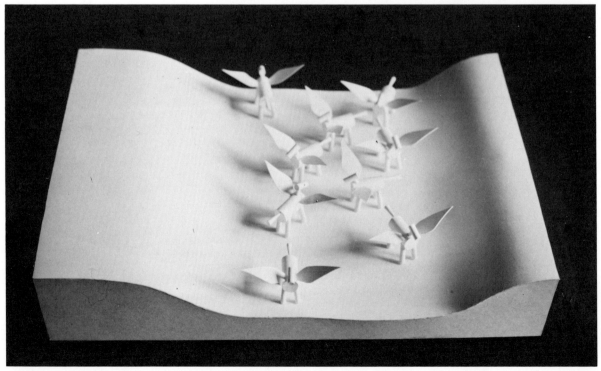

50

The forms shown here might be categorized as "wings with paper," for obvious reasons. John Billingham of New York City works in sizes that are almost miniature and are thus quite fascinating. Some of his inspiration comes from mythology. His piece at the top of the facing page is entitled "Timeo Danaos Et Dona Ferentes" (I fear the Greeks, even bearing gifts) and measures 11″ × 14″ × 18″ high. His "Pegasi in Depression", bottom, measures only 8½″ × 11″. Billingham writes, "I made nine Pegasi (relating to the nine Muses) in, literally, a depression implying a slow or stagnant period in my work." By extreme contrast, the large paper angel (above) flies among other Christmas ornaments at the Philadelphia College of Art. This angel was almost the size of the people who paused to enjoy it.

Wet and crumpled paper was explored as the technique for this sheep (facing page) by Ted Miller of Kramer, Miller, Lomden, Glassman graphic design group of Philadelphia. Artist-instructor Bill Crawford indulged in fantasy and intricate scissor work in the decorative piece shown above; the original is in brilliant color.

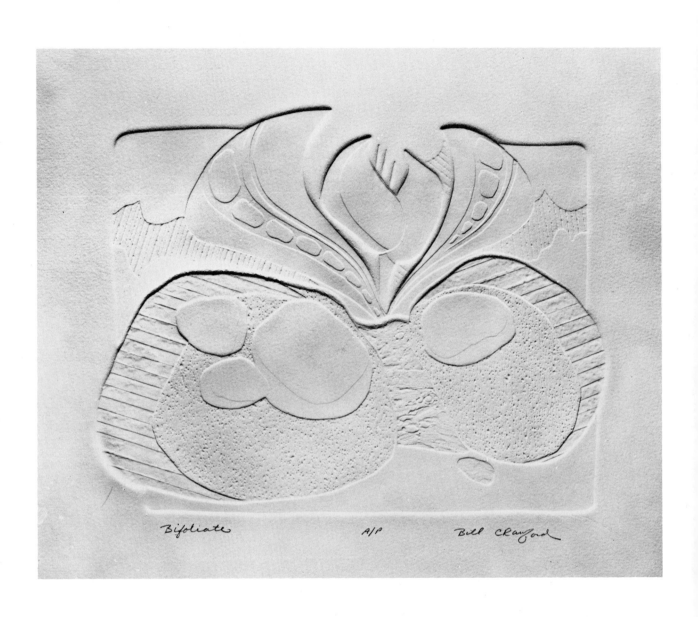

Bifoliate   A/P   Bill Crawford

Jeri Tom, October, 1977

The two hand-embossings, categorized as collographs in the fine arts world, have the same basic result as mechanical embossings in that the paper is molded to give dimensional form. Differing strikingly from his imaginative decoration, Bill Crawford was inspired by floral forms for his collograph (facing page). Jeri Tom went a step further than embossing by introducing a drawing of the foliage of a decorative house plant (above) that forms a relationship with the embossed forms.

Ever since its invention, paper and its usage have fascinated artists and craftsmen. During the 1970s there was a renaissance in the making of paper by hand; this involved many artists who then went on to use the material as an art medium. Two fine examples of the work of the distinguished artist Judith Ingram, of the Philadelphia area, are shown here. The piece on this page is entitled "Traces" and is of an edition of six. It measures 32″ × 26″ and is dated 1978. The piece on the facing page is entitled "Excelsior" and measures 24″ × 20″. It was designed in 1977 and is in the collection of Mrs. Howard Pressman of Swarthmore, Pennsylvania.

Three examples of handmade paper as art forms are shown here. These pieces were shown in 1979 at the Florence Duhl Gallery in New York City as part of an excellent exhibition entitled *Paper: Metamorphoses.* "Beach Grass & Mars Violet" (above) by Phyllis Peckar measures 26″ × 28″. Suzanne Adams designed the tall "Totem Six (right) which measures 40″ × 9″ × $2\frac{1}{2}$″. Both pieces are made of handmade paper, with the latter enclosing feathers and fiber. On the facing page is Robert Nugent's "Ancient Mariner Series," which he states is made of "handformed paper"; its dimensions are $17\frac{3}{4}$″ × $12\frac{3}{8}$″ × $1\frac{1}{4}$″.

59

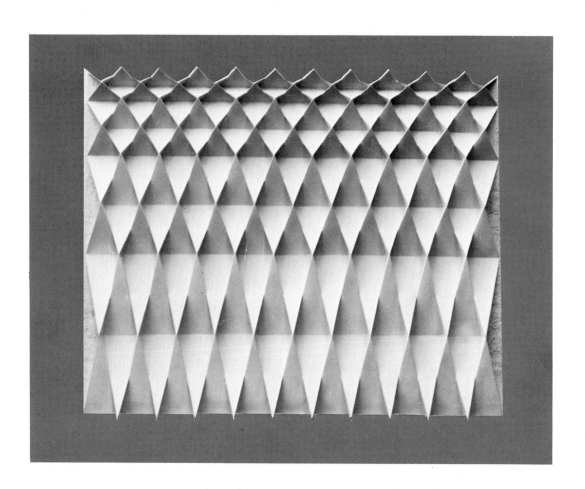

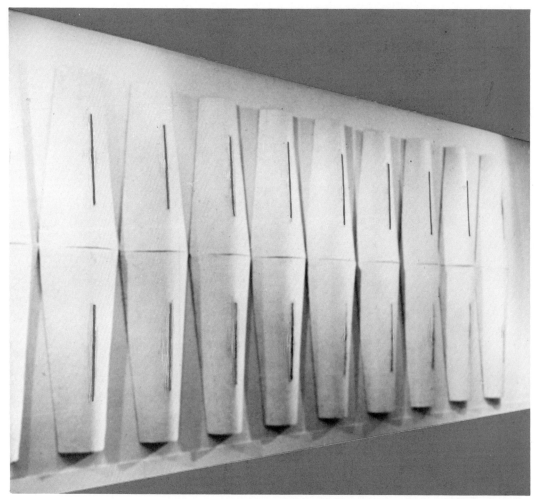

Bigness and boldness are the keynotes of the large pieces by the two artists represented here. Al Storz, whose studio is near Pottstown, Pennsylvania, is an artist/designer of many talents, among which are painting, drawing, sculpture, architectural design, packaging, and, of course, paper constructions (above and top of facing page). Douglas Zucco has been active as a designer and educator in the East, including Maryland and Georgia. He has exhibited widely and his work in paper is in large scale, appropriately used for wall hangings. The work shown at the bottom of the facing page is classified by the artist as a "handmade paper-cast 3-D wall piece." It measures 9′ × 28′ and is shown as exhibited at the Nexus Gallery in Philadelphia.

PAPER IN THE GRAPHIC ARTS

Graphic designers almost literally live with paper. They design on it, select the quality of paper needed for best results, design for the needs of reproduction and printing, and, as a continuation of this principle, should be involved with the character and weight of paper to be used for the printing. With newspaper, magazine, report, and other forms that involve pages, they are confined to the limits of size of the page itself and struggle to fulfill aesthetic and editorial requirements. But there are situations where graphic designers can break with the bounds of two-dimensional restrictions and can put to work many of the techniques that are shown on the following pages. Their ingenuity is then restricted only as far as reproduction mechanics, printing and mailing costs, and, of course, appropriateness for the assignment are concerned. Even these challenging limitations often lead to exceptional designs of lasting interest.

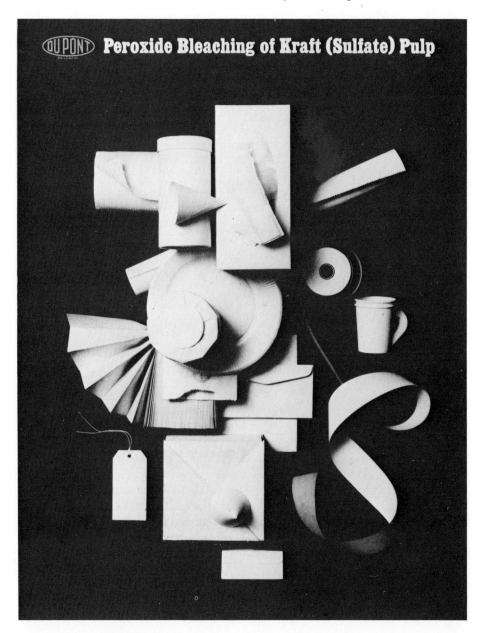

PERCRAFT CORPORATION
PERCRAFT PARK
TSBURGH, PENNSYLVANIA 15238

**Papercraft
1972 Annual Review**

The Papercraft Corporation of Pittsburgh, Pennsylvania, used this bold paper-sculpted sun face (above) on the front and back covers of its 1972 annual report. The art director was Ralph Marmo and the designer, Matthew T. Danko. It is the usual annual report size—$8\frac{1}{2}'' \times 11''$—and the cover is in lively vermillion, red, orange, and yellow. A photograph of white paper objects (facing page) is appropriately used in the design for the cover of a booklet about bleaching materials manufactured by E. I. du Pont de Nemours & Co., Wilmington, Delaware. The designers were Reese, Tomases & Ellick Inc. The size of this booklet is $8\frac{1}{2}'' \times 11''$.

MEET MR. PRINT

He's *your* man . . . calling on your prospects, selling to your customers. He's a low-budget traveling man you can send next door or half-way around the world for pennies. He never turns in an expense account; he never touches you for an advance. Yet he sells more goods and services than all his flesh-and-blood counterparts put together.

Mr. Print is a catalogue, a brochure, a direct mail piece, on duty 24 hours a day. He was created especially for you to sell your good and services. We create salesmen in print . . . and we put millions of them on the road every year selling everything from chairs to computers.

We can do the whole job right here in our shop . . . or any part of it. Idea men, artists, master printers—all work as a team. We can even mail it!

Put Mr. Print to work for you by returning the enclosed reply card today. Or telephone direct WAlnut 3-1945. (Area Code 215)

PRINTING SERVICES, INC.
919 Walnut Street
Philadelphia 7, Pa.

Three designs produced by cutting paper forms are shown here. "Mr. Print" (facing page) is an assemblage of paper forms in a poster by Samuel Maitin for Printing Services, Inc., both of Philadelphia, Pennsylvania. The art director was Frank Zachary. The poster is in full color and is $16\frac{1}{8}'' \times 21\frac{3}{8}''$. For the printing-paper sample-books (above) I designed a series of covers in which suggestive paper shapes became the design themes. The client was W. C. Hamilton & Sons, Miquon, Pennsylvania; the agency was Gray & Rogers, Philadelphia and Guy Fry was the art director. The sample-books measure $8\frac{1}{2}'' \times 11''$. In the designs for note papers shown below, Fred deP. Rothermel cut bold forms and used brightly colored papers. They were produced by Cordial Cards, Inc., Harrisburg, Pennsylvania.

Rolling or curling paper creates design potentials for artists and designers. In the cover and pages for an annual review (above) for Sperry Univac of Blue Bell, Pennsylvania, the presentation of the financial charts was enlivened by the curls of paper on which they appeared. The conception of this piece was by Allan Hill, art director and designer of Mandala, Inc. and the photography was by Seymour Mednick. The review measures $8\frac{1}{2}'' \times 11''$. Entirely different from the curl of paper on this page are accordion folds and "see through" die-cuts (facing page, top left) of a piece for the 1867 Exposition Universelle, Paris, France, now in the collection of the Cooper-Hewitt Museum of Design, Smithsonian Institution, New York. The contemporary piece (top right and bottom) for the New York Botanical Garden was designed by Roy Doty of West Redding, Connecticut. The original design concept—using only one sheet of paper—was by Carlton B. Lees.

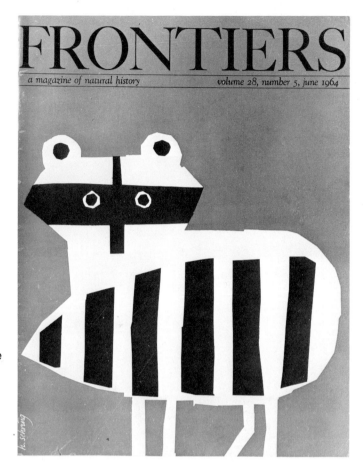

FRONTIERS

a magazine of natural history — volume 28, number 5, june 1964

Animal and bird forms are often used by artists as subjects; the examples shown here illustrate different applications of paperwork. The magazine cover (right) for the Academy of Natural Sciences of Philadelphia shows a surprised or, rather, surprising racoon; it was designed by Harry Sehring. I designed the playful papercut car card (below) with the assistance of Sol Cohen for the Philadelphia Zoo.

Peace on earth. Lois, Matt, Bobby, Beth and Jane Miller.

Ted Miller designed a greeting card (top left) using the paper cuts left by a paper punch to create the dove in flight; the card measures 9″ × 12″. After stacking a pile of 8½″ × 11″ paper and clamping it tightly, Don Madden of Ballston Springs, New York, drilled holes in it with an electric drill to form the contours of a reindeer (above).

VISIT THE PHILADELPHIA **ZOO**

OPEN DAILY
34th & GIRARD

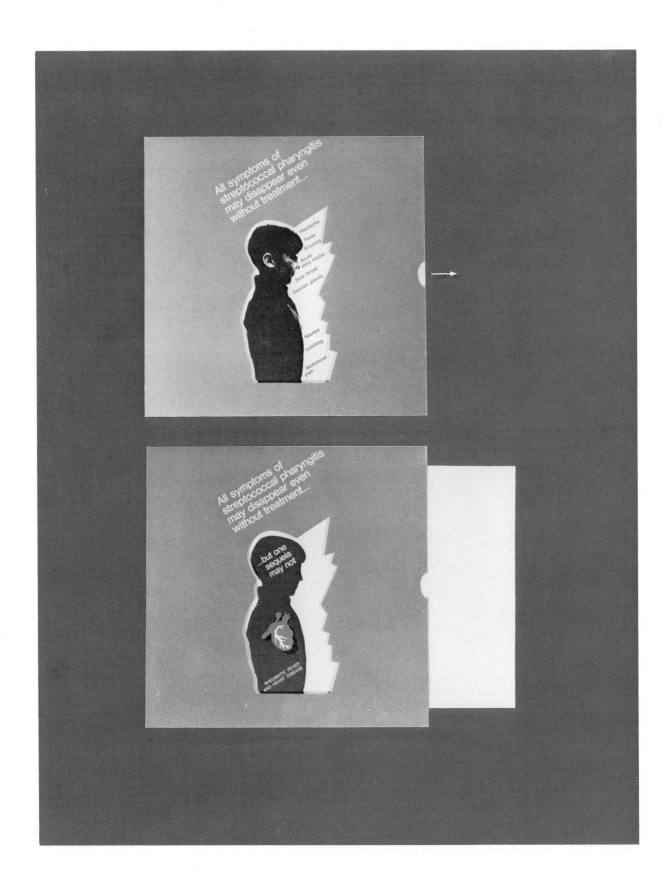

Graphic arts designs that make the recipient do something—pull-out, pop-out, form-up—are valuable because it is probable that the object may be kept or remembered for a longer time. The "pull-out" on the facing page shows only part of its message until the interior section is slipped out by pulling the tab for that purpose. The opening showing the boy is die-cut. This piece was conceived by the design team of Bruno Mease, Inc. for Wyeth International Limited of Radnor, Pennsylvania. The partridge in a pear tree greeting (top) is an example of a "pull-up" technique, one that may have been inspired by antique valentines (see page 19 for an example). The partridge was designed by Kramer, Miller, Lomden, Glassman for the Delaware Management Company, Inc., Philadelphia. It measures 10″ in diameter and about 5″ in height. Tom Vroman of Galeton, Pennsylvania, reminded clients and possible clients of his design organization's services by sending calendars (bottom) four times a year during 1980. Each calendar was mailed flat and had three creases for folding; it was up to the recipient to fold and paste one edge (prepasted) to produce a neat, triangular, three-month calendar.

PACKAGING FOR THINGS AND THOUGHTS

Packages of many sizes and shapes and materials are a part of our contemporary world. Paper and paperboard are very much in use and there are many organizations involved in the design and manufacture of packages using these products. Many packaging projects require the use of simple package forms involving squares, rectangles and cylinders. These forms are adequate but uninspired. They are often made more attractive by the graphics and decoration printed upon them. With ingenuity and imagination, forms for packaging can be made unusually interesting, sculpturally satisfying, and structurally superior. In the same way words and images can also be "packaged" to create a book. Books using different manners of presenting these words and images may be of unusual shapes and, in some cases, may literally burst open by the use of pop-ups, pop-outs, and pull-outs. These books bring enchantment to the eyes of a child (and to the grown-up, too). Direct-mail advertising material and instructional literature often employ similar techniques.

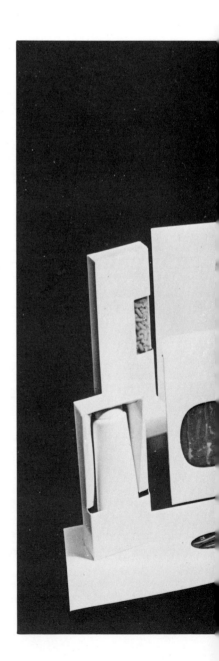

The large photograph at the right shows a variety of package forms reproduced in a handsome brochure entitled *Things Change*, published by the Container Corporation of America. This assemblage of suggested constructions indicates the immense variety of form and structure possible in packages made of white paperboard in a variety of weights. Two mock-ups for unusual package shapes (top right) exhibit the use of curved edges which are now possible in mass production. These packages were designed by the Structural Design Department of Container Corporation of America. A classic form (top left) in use for many years is exhibited in the Livana "Chocolate-Pear" package, which encloses an excellent product manufactured by Livana Cacao-Ges. Lindau M.B.H., Lindau-Bodensee, West Germany.

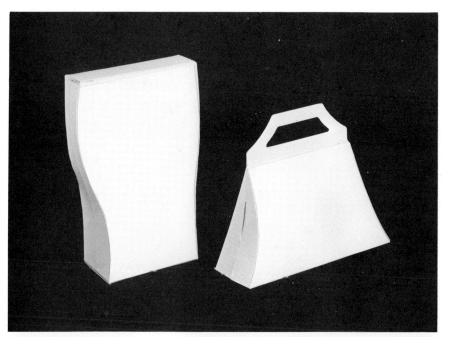

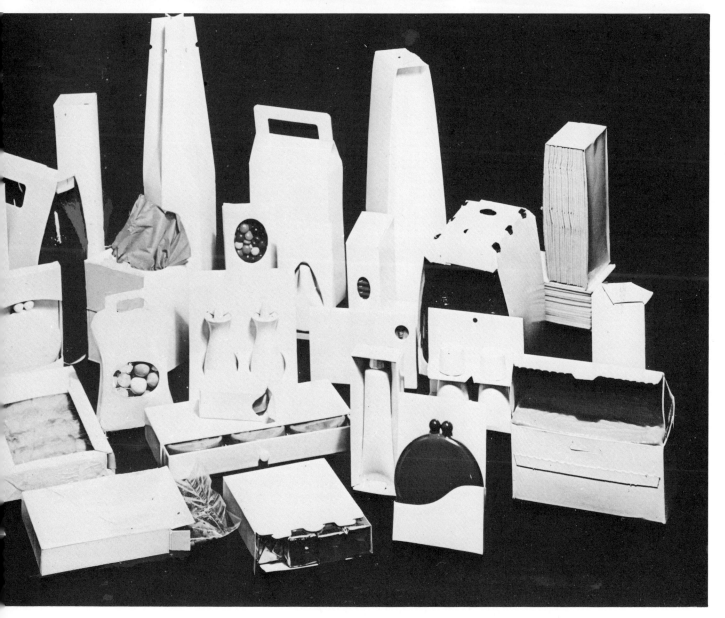

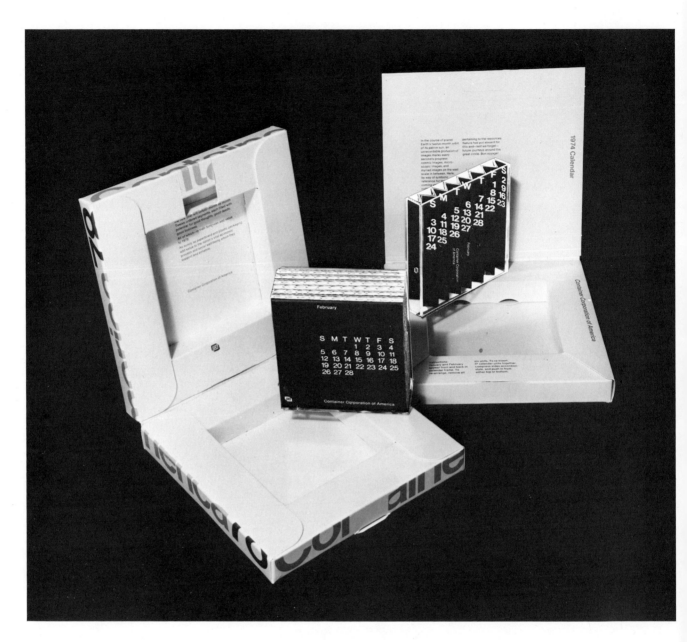

The handsomely designed and constructed packages above enclose unusual calendars sent out by the Container Corporation of America. The calendar forms are interesting constructions of paper or paperboard enclosed in small plastic cases. Similar in purpose is the package for another calendar, shown at the top of the facing page, which was sent by the same company. In this instance, the package and the form holding the calendar blocks are constructed of thin corrugated paperboard, which protects the calendar blocks and suggests the possible uses of corrugated board as an excellent design material. The calendar block itself is shown below (right). All of these packages were designed by the company's graphic designers and Kaulfuss Design, Chicago, Illinois.

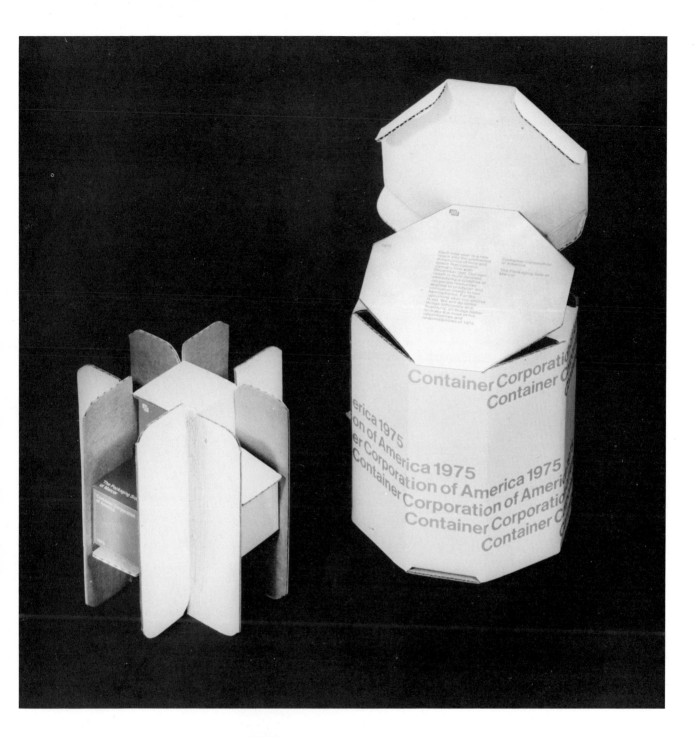

Holiday greetings sent by Arne Andersen of Denmark demonstrate unusual uses of paper. The one shown on this page comes in the form of a flat sheet into which the form of a dodecahedron has been stamped. When the recipient releases the cuttings and shapes them, the result is a twelve-sided, three-dimensional "package," with an intriguing and appropriate design or decoration on each side. The illustrations on the facing page show an unusual method of packaging a map. Tourists, especially motorists, who have battled with unwieldy maps will welcome the fold-out technique used for this one. The map is entitled "Bienvenues au Portugal" and was planned by an officer of the International Department of the Banco Nacional Ultramarino, Lisbon, Portugal.

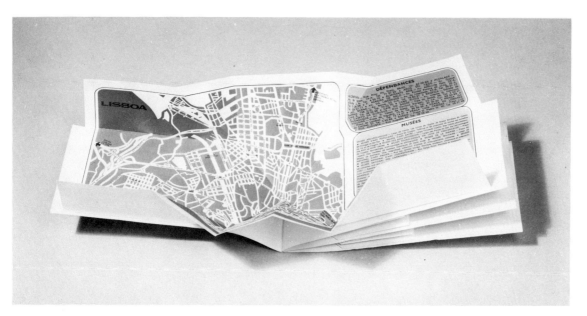

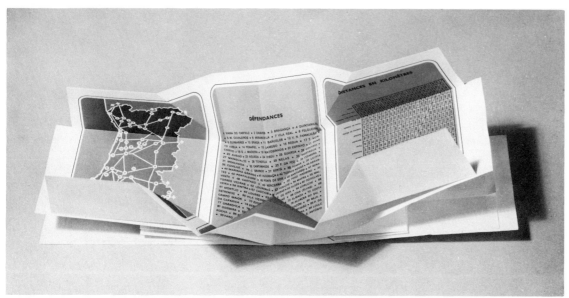

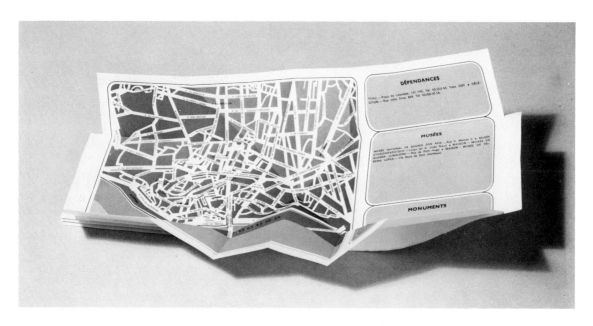

The concept of a book as a package for images and ideas is shown in the curved design of the pages cut to the shape of a fan for a book entitled *Painted Fans of Japan*. It was edited by Reiko Chiba and published by the Charles E. Tuttle Company of Rutland, Vermont, and Tokyo, Japan.

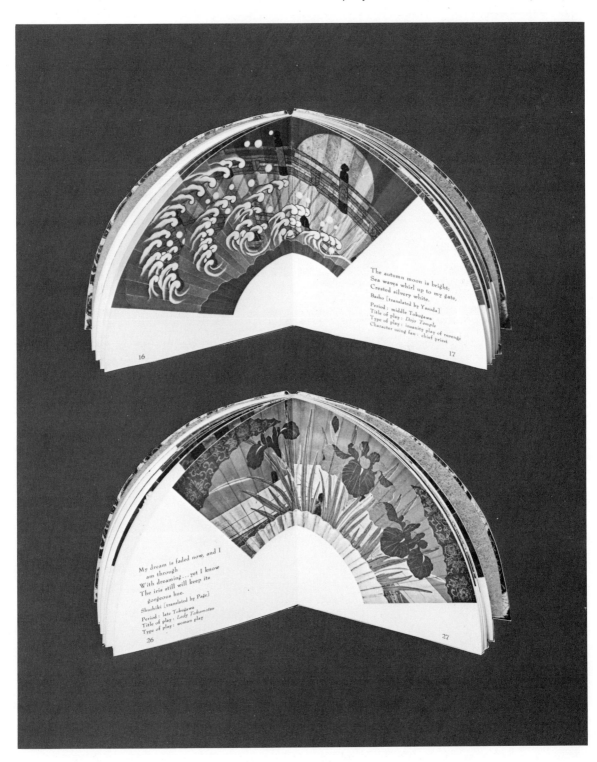

This unusual package opens to present a composite of paper textures, printing techniques, lavish color, and nine pop-up sections. *Bluebeard's Castle* was designed by Ron King and published by Circle Press Publications of Guildford, Surrey, England. The verses, which accompany each individual section, were written by Roy Fisher.

A blank, white-paper "dummy" (right) demonstrates how the pages of books are sometimes sliced to create interesting possibilities. An example of this is shown in a charming book entitled *Kellogg's Funny Jungleland Moving Pictures* (below) that I owned as a child. It was produced by the W. K. Kellogg Company of Battle Creek, Michigan, and was copyrighted in 1909. The animals' heads, bodies, and legs—as well as their costumes—become interchangeable when the various sections of the book are turned.

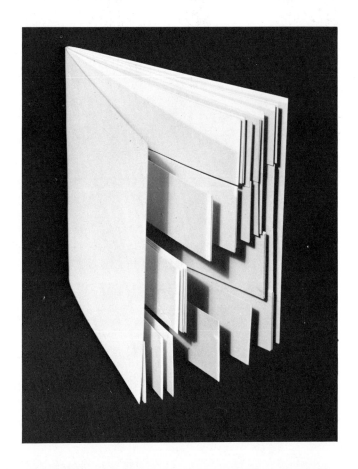

A handsome contemporary version of the cut-pages principle shown on the facing page is exhibited in a little book entitled *Heads, Bodies & Legs* by Denis Wirth-Miller and Richard Chopping. It was printed by Hunt, Barnard & Co. Ltd., Aylesbury, England, for Penguin Books, Inc. in 1946 and reprinted in 1951. Here again the figures and the exciting costumes change as the pages are turned.

The Great Menagerie is an adaptation of an antique pop-up book published in 1884 by J. F. Schreiber of Esslingen, Germany. It is in the collections of The Metropolitan Museum of Art, New York. The English language edition shown here was published in 1979 by the Museum and Penguin Books; it was produced by Intervisual Communications, Inc., Los Angeles, California. On the facing page are two out-of-print books of a series published by Bancroft & Co. (Publishers) Ltd., London, England, with illustrations by V. Kubavfa. These fabulous books create a tremendous visual and physical impact. Each opens with approximately eight pages of text followed by well-planned, well-constructed, and well-illustrated pop-ups of an Indian village in one example, and of Christopher Columbus's Santa Maria in the other.

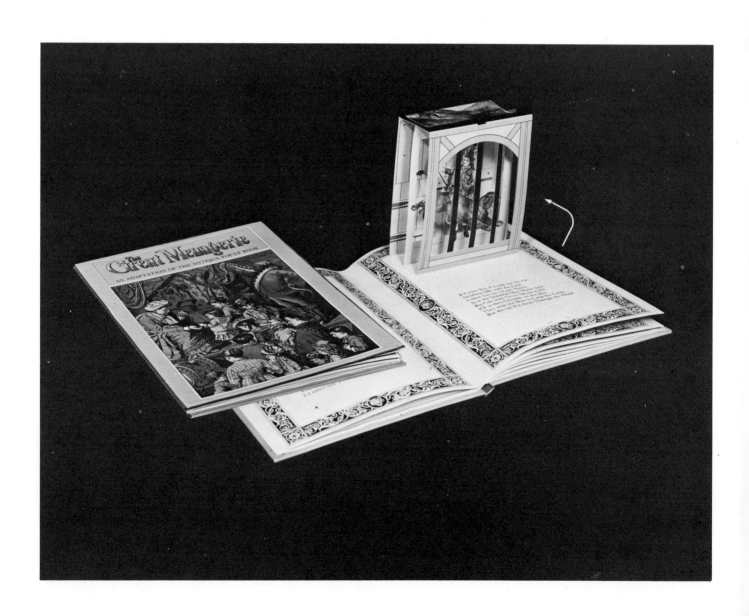

This fabulous antique "pop-up" book embodies accordion folds, die-cuts galore, pop-outs, and lavish circus colors. Its title is *International Circus* and, according to the text on the back cover, it "is considered the masterpiece of all Lothar Meggendorfer's pop-up books." A first edition was published in 1887 by J. F. Shreiber of Esslingen, Germany. There is a contemporary edition, published in 1979 by The Metropolitan Museum of Art, with whose permission the cover and the opened book are reproduced here. The book measures $8\frac{3}{4}'' \times 13''$ when closed and $52\frac{1}{4}''$ when fully opened. The pop-outs, with their die-cut figures and animals, extend forward about $4''$ from the background.

Arthur P. Williams, an artist and teacher, is also a collector of beautiful things, including fine books of unusual merit. The nostalgic and charming accordion-fold ABC book is from his collection. When fully opened out, the accordion spreads to 50¼"; the page for each letter of the alphabet measures 1 15/16" × 3 13/16". Also in Mr. Williams' collection is the contemporary accordion-fold book, *A Sunday In Monterey*, with woodcuts by the distin-

guished artist, Antonio Frasconi. This interesting little book was published by Harcourt
Brace Jovanovich, Inc., New York. Fully spread, the book measures an unbelievable
126″ (its breadth is not fully shown in the reproduction); each fold measures $2\frac{1}{8}″ \times 5\frac{3}{8}″$.
When completely folded the book fits neatly into a small cardboard slipcase.

Many terms might be used in describing this great accordion-fold book, but the word
spectacular is certainly appropriate. *A Shoal of Fishes*—Hiroshige is published
by The Metropolitan Museum of Art and is illustrated with forty pages of wood-
block prints that were first reproduced in Japan around 1832–33, (fourteen of the
prints in the book are in the collection of The Metropolitan Museum of Art in New York,
the gift of Mr. and Mrs. Bryan Holme). The introductory pages give information about
Andō Hiroshige (1797–1858) who was famous in Japan for his wood-block prints of
landscapes and other subjects. The book is reproduced here because of the masterful
use of paper. It is designed in accordion-folded pages rather than cut pages (each
double-spread being meticulously glued) and when this awe-inspiring book is fully
opened out, it measures over 32 feet. Supervisor of design and production of the book
was Margot Feeley.

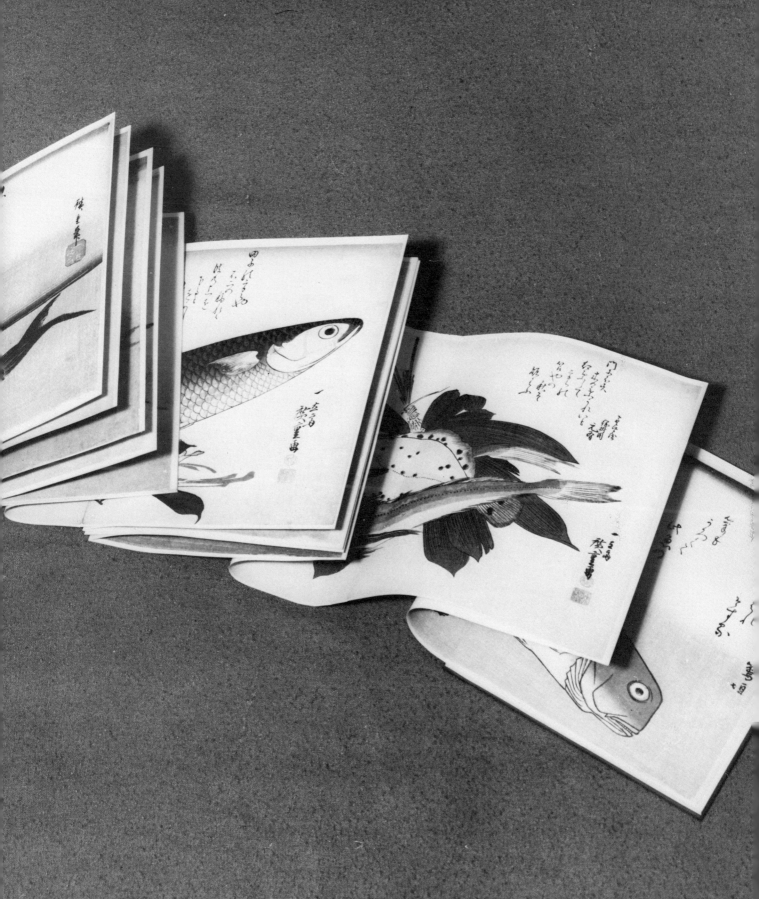

GEOMETRIC AND ABSTRACT FORMS

The work of the designers and architects in this section is based on geometrics, engineering, and architecture. Practitioners in these professions often choose paper for making models of their projects to explore the forms they might use for final constructions. The paper models, handsome in themselves, are also important in assisting clients to visualize the intended plans. The pieces shown here include both experimental work using paper to evolve abstract forms and more traditional applications.

1

2

Projects in dimensional work with paper are a part of the basic instructional programs of many art colleges. The excellent pieces shown here were produced by students in the foundation program at the Philadelphia College of Art under the direction of Edna Andrade, distinguished designer and painter. The designs on the facing page are by Sylvie Clement and on this page, reading clockwise from top left, by (1) Siri Korsgren, (2) Cheryl Ann Knowles, (3) Eric Johns, (4) Dane Fitch, and (5) Cheryl Mark.

5

3

4

Rea Ferdinand Hooker of New York City describes his handsome and surprising forms on this page as polyhedrons which may be rotated inwardly 360 degrees on an inter-vertical axis into five different positions and then returned to the original form. The pentagonal block, top left, can be raised into the polyhedron, left.

Top views (above and below) of two of the inner-rotated positions.

Correct positions (below) of the hands for three of the five inner-rotated positions.

The reproductions on this page show examples of Rea Ferdinand Hooker's inventions as applied to new structural concepts; these possess unique advantages as portable-temporary or prefabricated-permanent shelters. The illustrations below are from Mr. Hooker's excellent publication, *Innovations,* which explains possible uses for his structures. One of his models was constructed of 23 pt. paperboard, had a height of $3\frac{1}{2}''$, a diameter of $7''$, weighs less than two ounces, and would support 200 pounds evenly distributed on top.

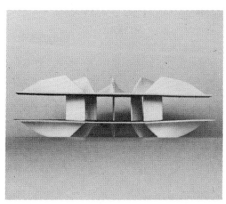

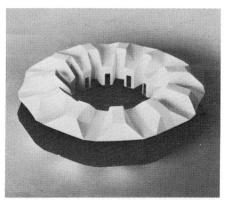

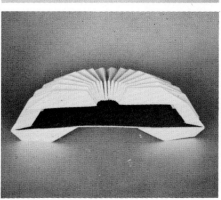

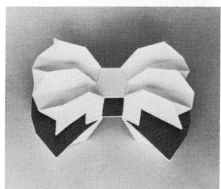

Franz Zeier, a teacher at the Kunstgewerbeschule der Stadt Zurich in Zurich, Switzerland, is well qualified to inspire young designers working with paper, as these very handsome examples of his talents indicate. The title of the design on this page is "Kubisches Raumgitter aus Oktaedern und Kuboktaedern" (Square [or cubic] Spatial Grid of Octahedrons and Cubes). The strikingly handsome pieces shown in the photograph on the facing page are entitled "Stelen" (Pillars).

Handsomely photographed to give the impression of sculpture, these models are made from paper tubes. They were designed by Robert Zeidman of Greenwich, Connecticut, a distinguished architect.

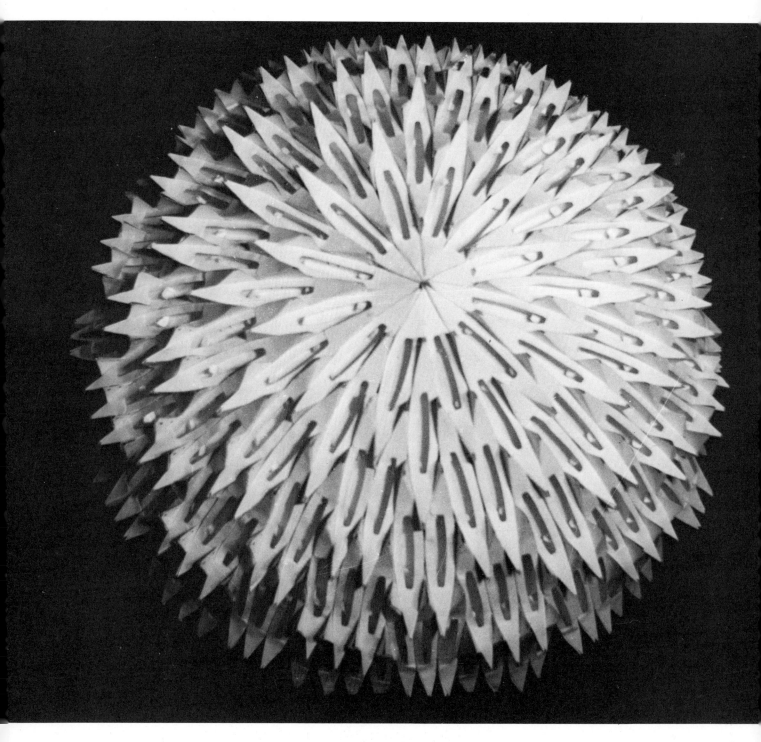

The striking objects shown on these and the next two pages were designed by Ernest R. Schaefer of Wayland, Massachusetts, an inventor, engineer, and sculptor, among other titles in an energetic career. Mr. Schaefer calls these designs "Dome Structures." In the design procedures Mr. Schaefer explains that "every unit is made of wax-coated fiberboard cut to the same pattern. This dome supports steel rods which fit through slits in the fiberboard while concrete is sprayed over the dome in a method called gunite. The outside is then smoothed and when the wax-coated forms are removed from the inside of the structure, an acoustical surface remains in reverse-molded concrete. The steel rods are for reinforcement within the concrete." All the dome models were constructed using Strathmore 2-ply paper.

"Dome #2" (above and page 100) was presented in a paper given at Yale University. Laminated paper, $\frac{5}{8}''$ thick is used to form a structure that has a span of 250 feet and can withstand 150 mph wind and snow load. Because the units fit inside one another the entire dome can be packed in eighteen boxes for easy shipment. Erection of the dome is quick and easy, starting from the base up without scaffolding. Each unit overlaps, preventing water from getting into the structure." The photograph on the next page is a view looking at the apex of Dome #2. Mr. Schaefer states, with proper pride, "There is no hardware or gluing or stapling of any kind in any of my structures; they are completely self-supporting."

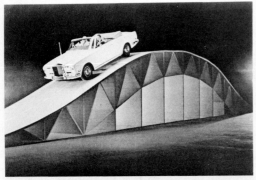

We drove this 2½ ton Rolls Royce over a bridge made entirely of St. Regis paper to prove a point.

The point is that paper can be stronger than you think. Especially if it's in the form of corrugated box material.

The roadbed of this bridge was made out of six layers of St. Regis triple-wall corrugated–a material we supply a lot of to the U.S. The verticals were made of five layers, and the triangles of four.

Triplewall is made up of three layers of the corrugated "medium" and four layers of linerboard. And it can withstand 1,100 lbs. per square inch of puncture pressure on its side. And on its edge, a 12 x 12 in. piece can take 930 lbs. A mere seven layers of paper!

The strength of corrugated isn't only in the paper itself. It's the structure. The shape of the medium is one of the strongest structures known. In Colonial Virginia walls were built in the corrugated, or serpentine form. And they're still standing today, although they're only one brick thick.

Corrugated box material is a sandwich. A wavy corrugated medium is squeezed between two rollers with meshing teeth. That's the meat of the sandwich. The bread is two layers of heavy paper called linerboard.

Since it was patented in 1871, corrugated has been one of the mainstays of the American distribution system. In fact, the corrugated box is one reason we have the most efficient distribution system in the world.

And St. Regis has had its share of innovations in the field. Partly because we're one of the largest makers of linerboard in the world. And partly because of our technology and marketing thrust.

All this reflects the marketing stance of St. Regis toward all our packaging, paper, lumber and construction products. To use the full weight of our technology in serving our markets and in renewing the forest resource our products come from.

St. Regis—serving Man and Nature.

We drove this 2½ ton Rolls-Royce over a bridg

The point is that paper can be stronger than you think. Especially if it's in the form of corrugated box material.

The roadbed of this bridge was made out of six layers of triple-wall corrugated—a material which St. Regis is a major producer of. The verticals were made of five layers, and the triangles of four.

Triplewall is made up of three layers of the corrugated "medium" and four layers of linerboard, as shown below. And it can withstand 1,100 lbs. per square inch of puncture pressure on its side. And on its edge, a 12 x 12 in. piece can take 930 lbs. A mere seven layers of paper!

What makes corrugated so strong?

The strength of corrugated isn't only in the paper itself. It's the structure. The shape of the medium is one of the strongest structures known. In Colonial Virginia walls like the one shown here, we built in the corrugated, or serpentine form And they're still standing today, although they're only one brick thick.

The greatest strength of corrugated is the vertical direction, where, as long as it maintains the vertical— which the box shape tends to help it do—it will support phenomenal weights.

How corrugated is made.

Corrugated is a sandwich. A wavy corrugated medium is squeezed between two rollers with meshing teeth as shown on the right. That's the meat o sandwich. The bread is layers of heavy paper ca linerboard. These three glued together and the resu one of the strongest and most ver packaging materials around.

Of course, you can also make corruga with two, or even three layers of medium—

Paper and paper products can be surprisingly strong.
The St. Regis Paper Company of New York City built this
bridge of corrugated box material and ran a 2½-ton
automobile over it to prove its strength. These two
advertising pages are shown courtesy of the company.

...ade entirely of St. Regis paper to prove a point.

did for our bridge. And the mediums in our ...plewall are a combination of different ...cknesses.

New wrinkles for corrugated.

Since it was patented in ...71, corrugated has been ...e of the mainstays of the Ameri- ...n distribution system. In fact, the ...rrugated box is one reason we ...ve the most efficient distribution system in ...e world. With it you can ship products over ...e exceptionally long distances we have in ...s country, efficiently and cheaply.

St. Regis has had its share of innovations in ...e field. Partly because we're one of the largest ...kers of linerboard in the world. And partly ...cause of our technology and marketing thrust.

And we're finding a lot of new uses for ...rrugated. We're out to replace more expen- ...e packaging. One of its greatest advantages ...hat, unlike packaging made of steel or wood, ...can ship our boxes flat to the customer. So ...aves on shipping costs.

Technology and marketing.

All this reflects the marketing stance of

St. Regis toward all our packaging, paper, lumber and construction products. To use the full weight of our technology in serving our markets and in renewing the forest resource our products come from.

Serving Man and Nature to the benefit of both.

103

104

Architects often make paper or paperboard models of proposed building and project designs for their clients. The two models on these pages were designed by Mitchell/Giurgola Architects of Philadelphia and New York. In addition to being handsomely executed, the model on the facing page is interesting in its use of paper patterns which suggest materials to be used in construction. Particularly unusual is

the model for a contemporary-style suburban home (above), because
even the trees have been designed with paper. The photographs are
by Rollin R. La France.

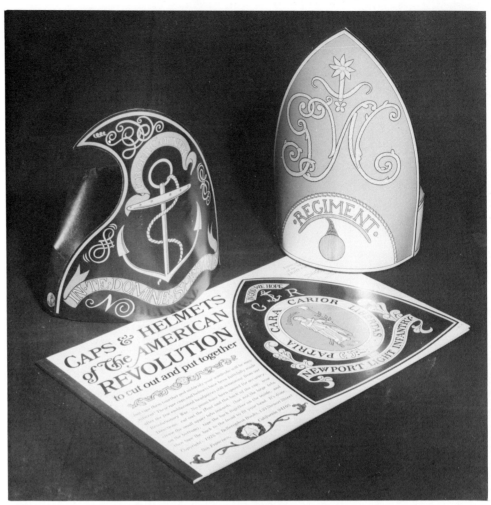

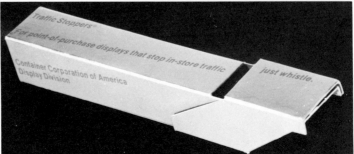

106

DO-IT-YOURSELF

The paper objects shown on these two pages may be considered "do-it-yourself" pieces. *Caps & Helmets of the American Revolution* (Bellerophon Books, Santa Barbara, California, c. 1980) comes as a large, white, paperboard book measuring 17" × 11". The regimental-hat forms are printed in color and can be cut out and constructed. The one at the top of the facing page is 12" tall when formed.

Thomas Vroman of Thomas Vroman Associates, Inc. of Galeton, Pennsylvania, is a talented and prolific designer who often does unusual things with paper. He designed the pieces shown below for Abbott Laboratories of North Chicago, Illinois, in conjunction with art director Charlie Walz. The package contains a set of ten sheets from which various colorfully designed figures, animals, and circus objects can be formed. The do-it-yourself set was related to a product named Compocillin, and William R. Sample, also an art director at Abbott, writes, "The original intent was to offer the parent or guardian of a child something to occupy the child during a 10-day medication regimen when rest and quiet are extremely beneficial."

Container Corporation of America produced the do-it-yourself cap, shown on the facing page, center, as a promotion piece. By turning the edges of the brim, it becomes a cap by means of the ingenious die-cut swirls. And, believe it or not, the paper whistle shown with the cap *does* whistle. Both were created by the company's structural and graphic designers.

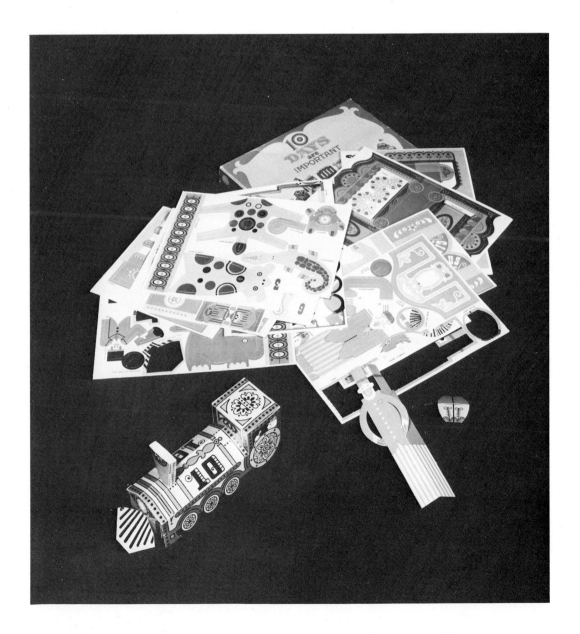

Die-cutting and folding techniques are demonstrated in the pieces shown on these two pages. The handsome bird winging its way across the top of the facing page is an English male merlin, known in America as the pigeon hawk; it is made entirely of paper. This bird is one of a series designed by Malcolm B. G. Topp of Sussex, England, for his *Birdmobile Card Sculptures*. A partly assembled merlin is shown with an envelope which contains the flat sheets from which the parts of the birds are cut before assembly. On this page is another fine example of paper assemblage. The model of Old North Church in Boston may be assembled by anyone patient and skilled enough to do so. This fine piece is one of several paper-structure *Landmark Models* from Ocko Associates, Inc., Brookline, Massachusetts. The design was by Stephen J. Ocko and the illustration by Stephen A. Rettew.

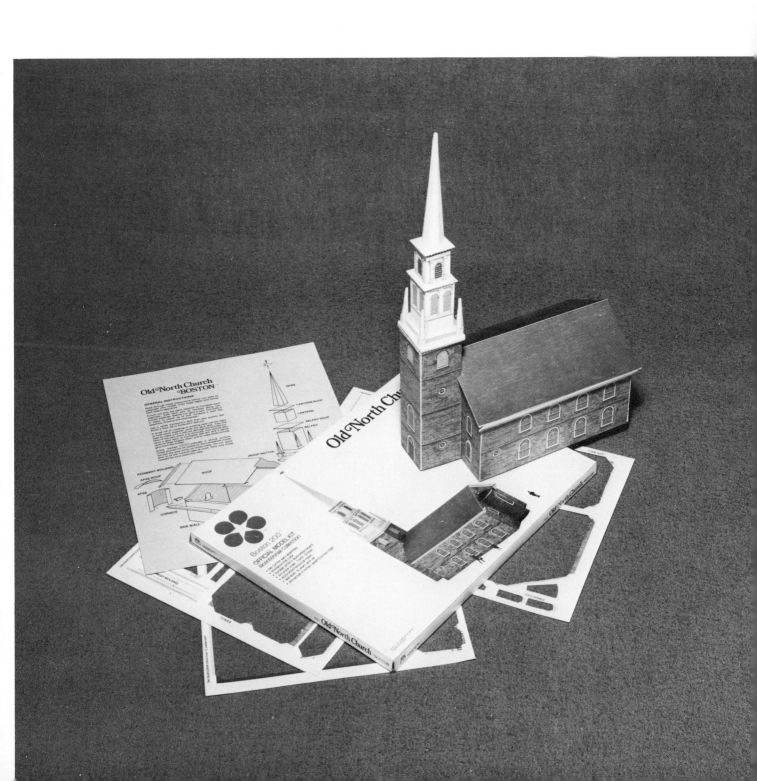

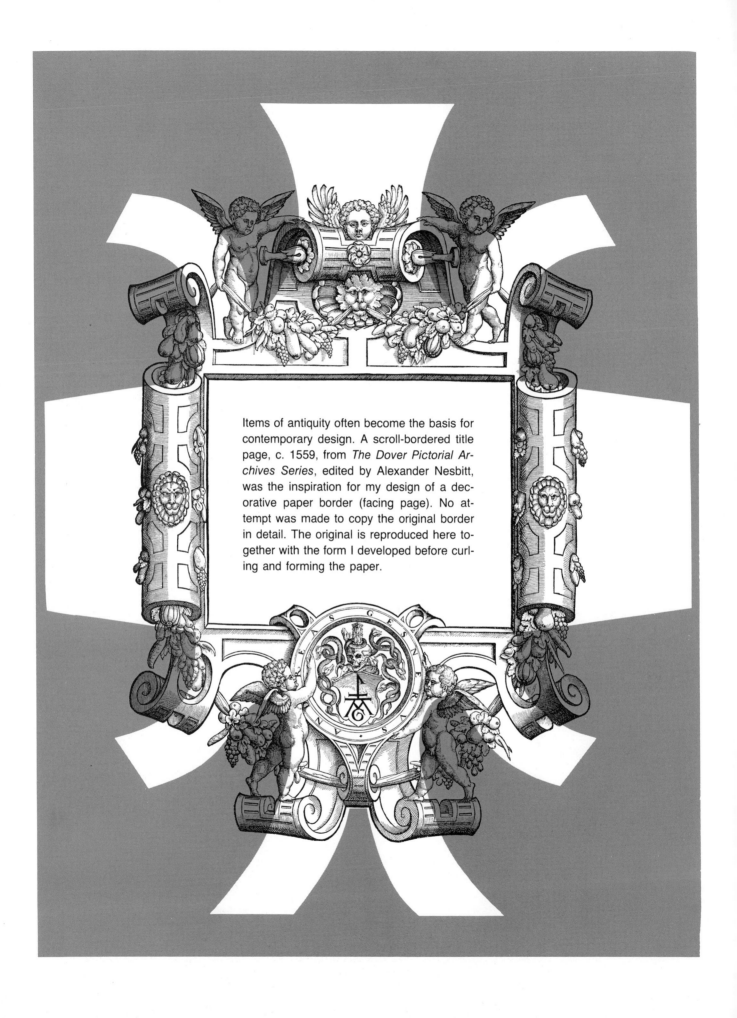

Items of antiquity often become the basis for contemporary design. A scroll-bordered title page, c. 1559, from *The Dover Pictorial Archives Series*, edited by Alexander Nesbitt, was the inspiration for my design of a decorative paper border (facing page). No attempt was made to copy the original border in detail. The original is reproduced here together with the form I developed before curling and forming the paper.

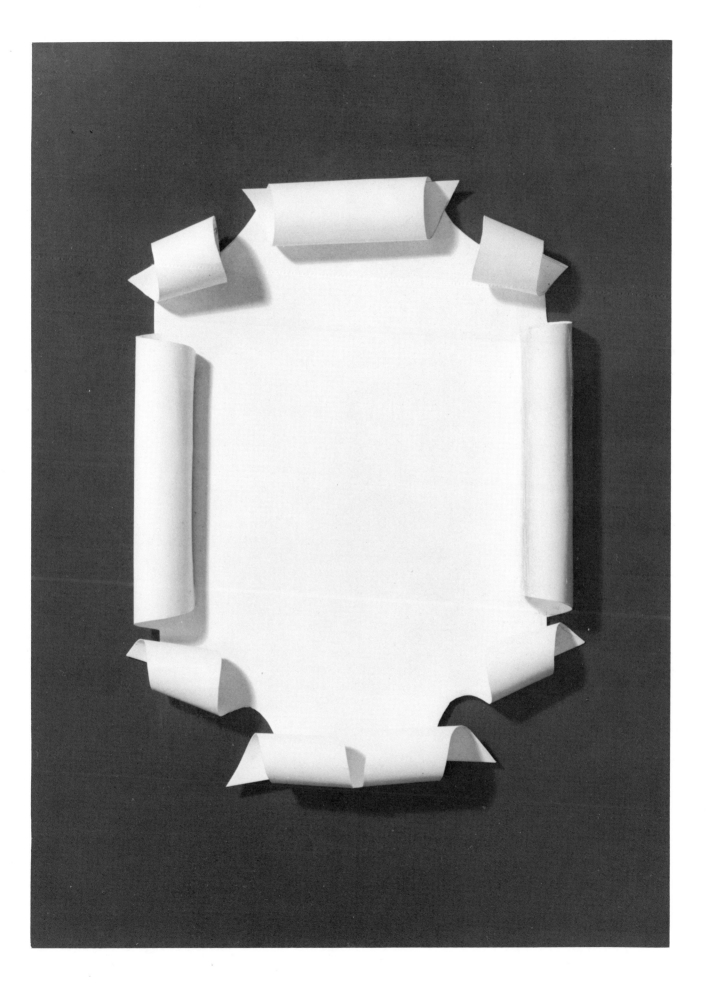

Carol Guida is a Philadelphia architect whose train-
ing included projects in construction and materials.
The assignment for a wine-bottle hanger made entirely of corrugated board required that no glue, sta-
ples, or other fasteners be used in its design. The
use of the corrugated board was appropriate because
of its strength and ability to be formed around bottles.

VARIATIONS IN PAPER

The last section of this book is devoted to a miscellany of works in paper. While the examples shown here may embody any of the techniques outlined in previous sections, they are too varied to categorize in a simple manner. The exhibits may range from unusual items in papier mâché to exquisitely detailed delicate boxes, from things that fly in the air to large furniture—all in paper. A great variety of *kinds* of paper—for instance, corrugated board and heavier fibers—may be found here because of the nature of the designed items. Most important to note is the fact that the designers had no rules or instructions to follow in devising their conceptions, thus increasing the need for the use of the word *miscellaneous*.

In the middle and late 1800s, hat boxes and band boxes, usually constructed with cardboard, were covered with decorative paper—often wallpaper—to protect the hats that adorned the heads of those days. Some of the shapes of the hats can be determined by the shapes of the boxes. The box at the lower left is known as a "band box"; it held hats as well as other items of apparel, such as gloves and scarves. The hat boxes and the band box are in the collection of and shown by courtesy of The Henry Francis du Pont Winterthur Museum, Winterthur, Delaware.

On the facing page are some hats made of newspaper which also have traditions. In newspaper plants, typesetters and pressmen have frequently taken unused sheets of newspaper and folded them into simple hats. These newspaper hats, though unstylish, protected hair from the grease of the composing and printing rooms. James Smart, writer, editor, and publisher, prepared the hats shown here.

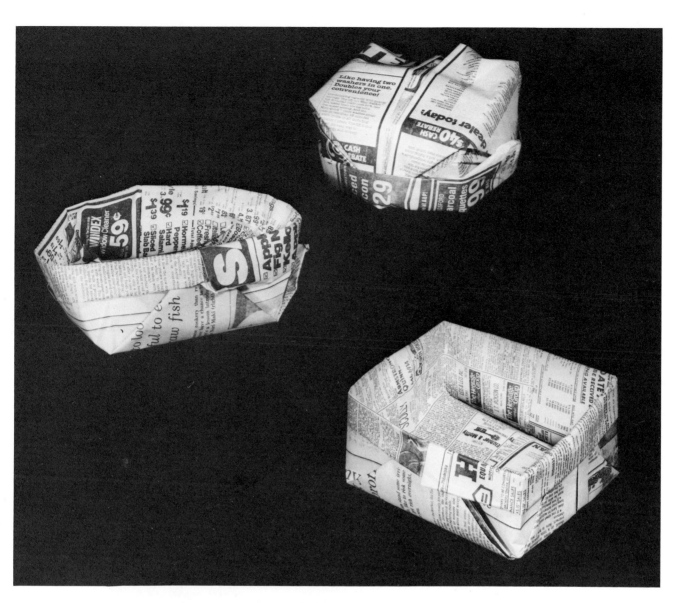

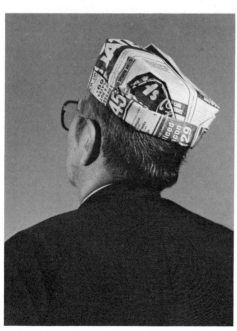

Papier-mâché has been used for ceremonial, processional, theatrical, and even battle and warfare accoutrements, particularly for masks. The huge tiger's head (above) from India is a ceremonial head mask and fits easily over the head of an adult. At the top left of the facing page is an ancient demon Nō mask used by actors in traditional Japanese theatre. To its right is a strange piece from India called a hood mask. Masks often have traditional meanings. Chinese painted masks were originally used in the fields of battle to frighten the enemy; later they were adopted for theatrical purposes. The mask at the bottom (right) is a contemporary version of a Chinese face-painting mask. The masks shown here are from the collection of Dr. and Mrs. Mayo Bryce.

Two surprising paper pieces are shown on this page. The 1844 English side chair is made of papier-mâché with gilt decoration and mother-of-pearl inlay. It was a gift of Mr. and Mrs. Arthur Weisberger to the Cooper-Hewitt Museum of Design in New York, by whose kind permission it is shown here. The round box, unbelieveably made of papier-mâché, is $3\frac{5}{16}''$ in diameter and dates 1814–1850; the portrait engraving is by David Edwin after a painting by Rembrandt Peale. It is in the collection of The Henry Francis du Pont Winterthur Museum in Winterthur, Delaware.

The "Paper House in Pigeon Cove, Massachusetts," is truly a house made of old newspaper. The walls, a clock, chairs, furniture, and even the fireplace are of paper. The photographs are reproduced by courtesy of Mrs. S. M. Curtis.   119

Architect Frank O. Gehry's method of laminating corrugated cardboard in several layers produces furniture with strong, rollicking curves and straight angles. Surprisingly, lit cigarettes left on the surface of this furniture will not burn it. Mr. Gehry, head of Frank O. Gehry and Associates Inc. of Santa Monica, California, is in the forefront of designers experimenting with unusual uses of paperboard for various products. The photographs are by Gordon Sommers.

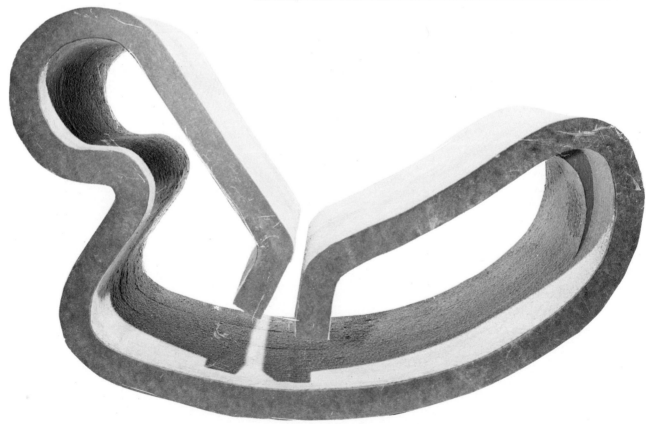

Designed by the Prestfibre staff of British Molded Fibre Ltd., Reading, England, and manufactured by the same company, this "Mohow" sectional playhouse (above) measures 40″ high × 46″ in diameter. British Molded Fibre Ltd. also produces such products as the truck door panel shown below.

Ed Rossbach of Berkeley, California, is the creator of the plaited newspaper constructions shown on this page and reproduced by permission of *Craft Horizons* magazine (April 1972 issue). "An Irrelevant Solution" (bottom left) measures 11″ × 12″ × 12″. "Soft Construction" (bottom right) measures 24″ × 20″ × 17″. Above these is a detail of "An Irrelevant Solution." I had a bit of fun with paper for the piece shown on the facing page. Here a single sheet of one-ply bristol was printed with the word *jitters* and cut into strips, which were shifted up and down in position to enhance the "jittery" idea.

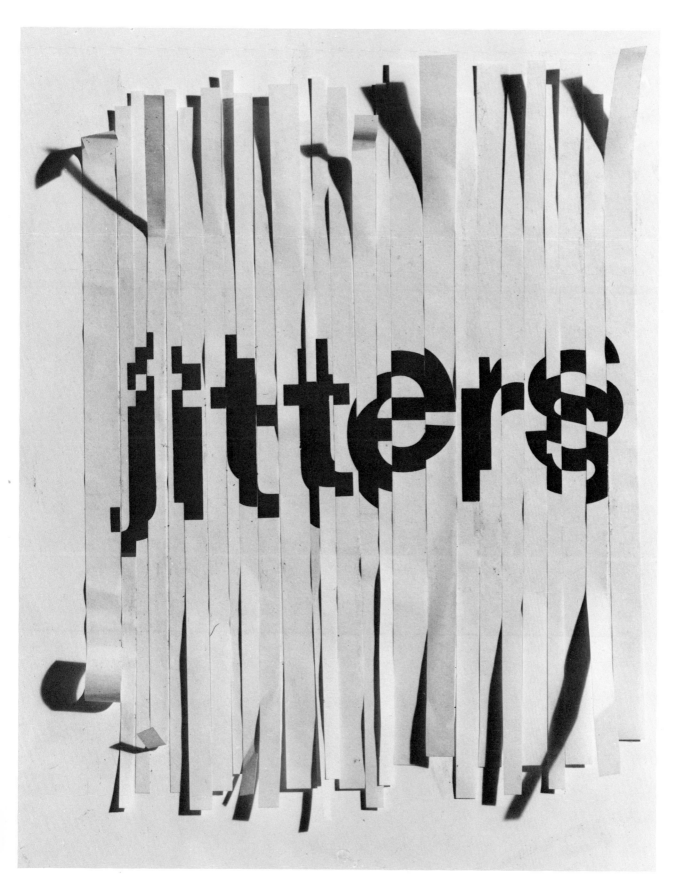

123

There is no object made of paper more commonplace than a paper bag. The "Tote Bags" designed and distributed by The Gordon Fraser Gallery, Ltd. of Newtown, Connecticut, are very distinctive. These are ordinary string-handle paper bag forms embellished with appealing decorations. They are certainly a handsome way to transport a bottle of wine or other gift to a friend. The art director was Clair Bannister and the designer of the totes was Adrienne Samuelson.

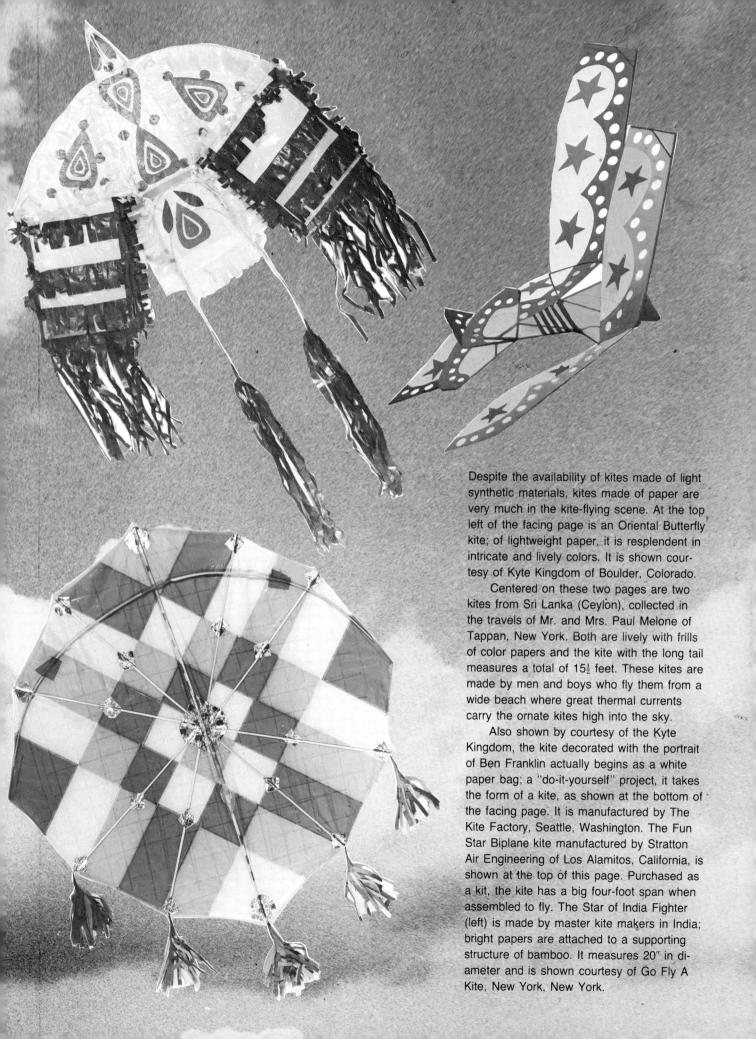

Despite the availability of kites made of light synthetic materials, kites made of paper are very much in the kite-flying scene. At the top left of the facing page is an Oriental Butterfly kite; of lightweight paper, it is resplendent in intricate and lively colors. It is shown courtesy of Kyte Kingdom of Boulder, Colorado.

Centered on these two pages are two kites from Sri Lanka (Ceylon), collected in the travels of Mr. and Mrs. Paul Melone of Tappan, New York. Both are lively with frills of color papers and the kite with the long tail measures a total of 15½ feet. These kites are made by men and boys who fly them from a wide beach where great thermal currents carry the ornate kites high into the sky.

Also shown by courtesy of the Kyte Kingdom, the kite decorated with the portrait of Ben Franklin actually begins as a white paper bag; a "do-it-yourself" project, it takes the form of a kite, as shown at the bottom of the facing page. It is manufactured by The Kite Factory, Seattle, Washington. The Fun Star Biplane kite manufactured by Stratton Air Engineering of Los Alamitos, California, is shown at the top of this page. Purchased as a kit, the kite has a big four-foot span when assembled to fly. The Star of India Fighter (left) is made by master kite makers in India; bright papers are attached to a supporting structure of bamboo. It measures 20″ in diameter and is shown courtesy of Go Fly A Kite, New York, New York.

R.S.V.P.

The six intricate and handsome forms shown on the facing page can hardly be called experiments in the true sense of the word. They are, rather, an exhibition of the great technical facility of graphic artist Brian De Frees of Manayunk, Pennsylvania. Each letter is box-like in character and decorated with delicate designs cut from white bristol board; the originals are slightly larger than these reproductions. They suggest the possibility of embossing on small packages.

Experimentally rolling and curling strips of light bristol board, I developed the design, shown on this page, for the border of an imaginative RSVP card. In order to gain control of the curling paper, the design was quite large—22″ × 24½″.

In the hands of designers paper is a useful medium for exhibition and display purposes. The two examples of exhibition pieces in paper, shown on the facing page, are from the 1946 "Britain Can Make It" Exhibition, courtesy of the Design Council of London. A section of the exhibition, "Things For Children," was designed by James Gordon; the ornate paper cake and the flowers were designed and executed by Tadeusz Lipski, a distinguished Polish artist. The toy theatre from the same exhibition was designed by Mr. Lipski and K. Griffin for "Shop Window Street."

Heraldry and crests have long been a part of the British scene and have been produced in various mediums. Tadeusz Lipski designed the handsome one reproduced above in paper in conjunction with the "Britain Can Make It" Exhibition.

This heraldic piece, quite large in size, was photographed in the lounge of an airlines ticket office in London, England. It was made with shiny papers, mostly in silvers and golds, and gave great distinction to a large blank wall. The decorative piece on the facing page was done for no purpose at all. It might be classified as a whimsy by artist-designer Bill Crawford, whose designs in paper show his delight in working with paper as a medium.

This magnificent German Village, "Model-Bogen," was published as a "do-it-yourself" project by Scholz Mainz Verlag, Munich, West Germany. The printing of this village has been discontinued, but similar pieces are now made by Verlag J.F. Schreiber, Esslingen, West Germany, and distributed by Handcraft From Europe of Sausalito, California. These authentic and beautifully printed cutout paper models are marked with clear instructions for cutting, folding, and construction, but require patience and skill to put together.

The miniature white church (above) was designed by
Arthur P. Williams of Philadelphia. It was a prototype for
similar churches produced in paper and used for the dis-
play of DeBeers diamond wedding rings. The hanging
Christmas decorations (right) were designed and cut by
Fred deP. Rothermel. In 1964, some of Mr. Rothermel's
pieces were included in the Christmas decorations in the
White House, Washington, D.C.

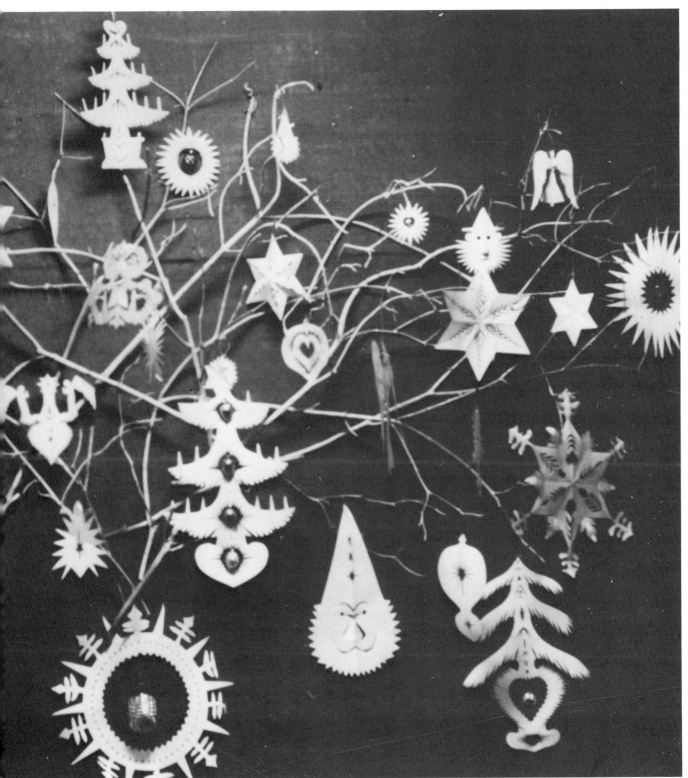

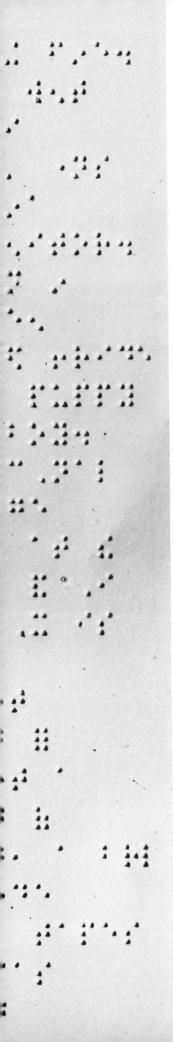

One of the most unusual and benevolent uses of paper is the Braille system of writing for the blind, devised by Louis Braille, a blind French student, in 1824. It consists of a series of raised dots placed in six-part cells; the full system involves sixty-three patterns.

Other methods had been in use before Braille developed his dot system, one of which simply used embossed forms of the Roman alphabet enlarged for touch-scanning; since the reader had to realize the form of the total character, this system was obviously slow and tedious. Therefore, despite opposition from sighted teachers, who insisted that it was absurd to try to teach an alphabet that was not based on the raised Roman alphabet, blind students eagerly embraced the new system. But it was not until thirty years later that Braille was officially adopted, with modifications to suit the needs of many languages.

In addition to its practical application, a page of Braille has a rich, artistic effect—an effect that has been at least partially captured by the photograph on the facing page—and it is a use of paper that is a source of understanding, learning, and joy for so many people which should certainly be included here.

It is not economically feasible to include a page of actual Braille in a book of this nature and, therefore, only photographic reproduction is shown at left. The original page of Braille was especially prepared with the permission of Richard Riddell, Librarian, Library for the Blind and Physically Handicapped, Free Library of Philadelphia. It was typed by Susan Clardy and photographed by Thomas J. Laverty.

139

GLOSSARY

This glossary of terms used in relation to paper is mainly concerned with names and terms in contemporary usage. Many terms used in the making of paper, both traditional and contemporary, handmade and manufactured, may not be found here and should be sought in books particularly related to papermaking processes. A few of these are listed in the Bibliography.

A **Against the grain.** Paper folded at right angles to the grain
Antique finish. Paper having a natural, rough finish

B **Basic weight.** The designation given to a paper in terms of the weight of 500 sheets (one ream)
Beater, Hollander. A machine developed in Holland in the late seventeenth century for "beating" or shredding pulp in the process of papermaking
Blind embossing. A term applied to embossing without the use of ink or foil
Bond paper. A strong paper generally used for business purposes, letterheads or forms, for example
Book paper. A paper, used for books, catalogs, and periodicals, with characteristics delineated as antique, vellum, machine-finished, coated, etc.
"Broke." A term applied to handmade but imperfect paper; also called "retree" and "outsides"
Bristol. A grade of paper particularly useful for artists and designers; available in "plies" (single-ply, two-ply, etc.) and with both soft and hard surfaces

C **Calendared paper.** The name applied to a high-gloss paper achieved by passing the paper between calendar rolls
Cast coated paper. A high-gloss enamel finish achieved by rolling a coated paper against a polished cylinder under pressure
Cold press. A paper or board that has been made without heat and thus has a dull surface; a term applied to bristol and illustration boards (see Hot press)
Collograph. A hand-embossed art print
Cover-weight paper. A somewhat heavier weight of paper often specified for covers in printing, as opposed to text-weight paper, which is thinner and lighter
Crash finish. A paper finish similar to coarse linen
Cut-outs. Printed die-cut pieces having irregular shapes
Cutscore. A sharp-edged knife used in die-cutting; usually several thousandths of an inch lower than the cutting rules in a die and used to cut part way into a paper or board for folding purposes

D **Dandy roll.** A wire cylinder mounted on papermaking machines that produces woven or laid effects as well as watermarks on paper
Debossing. A process in which lettering or art forms are pressed *into* the paper (or other material), creating a sunken image on the surface (see Embossing)
Deckle edge. Untrimmed or feathered edge of a sheet of paper; originally considered an imperfection, now often produced to get a special handmade look in paper
Die-cut. A process that results in shapes or forms being cut in paper as part of a printing project
Dummy. A "mock-up" of a proposed page or design that gives the effect of a final piece
Duplex paper. Paper having a different color on each side

E **Eggshell.** A term applied to paper with a finish resembling the surface of an egg
Embossing. Imposing letters or art forms in relief in paper (or other materials); results in raised surfaces
Enamel. A high-gloss surface on coated paper
English finish. Smooth-finished, calendared, machine-made paper used primarily in book work

F **Fabriano.** Italian paper manufacturer first mentioned in the history of papermaking in 1276 and magnificent-quality handmade papers still available under this famous name
Felt side. The top side of the sheet of paper in papermaking; the preferred side for printing
Fibers. The result of macerating pulp in the first step of papermaking
Fourdrinier. Papermaking machine, sponsored by the Fourdrinier brothers in England about 1800, that manufactures most grades of paper
French fold. The name applied to an eight-page folder printed on one side; used to gain added bulk and an impressive appearance and often embossed or die-cut
Fuzz. Lint or loose fibers appearing on the surface of paper

G **Grain.** The direction of the fibers in a sheet of paper

H **Hot press.** A sheet of paper with a very smooth surface created by the application of heat in manufacture (*see* Cold press)
Hot stamping. Impressions of gold, silver, or other bright colors achieved by applying heat and pressure to foils

I **India paper.** A paper with a very light buff color

K **Kraft paper.** A strong, usually brown paper generally used for bags and wrapping paper; sometimes attractively used in the graphic arts

L **Laid paper.** A paper with parallel lines running at right angles to chain marks, which run with the grain, made by a dandy roll
Laminated. Formed in thin layers which adhere to and are mounted on each other, as in paper or paperboard
Ledger paper. A strong, smooth paper used for bookkeeping and business purposes, hence its name
Linen-finish paper. A paper with a surface that gives the effect of linen fabric

M **Maceration.** The process of breaking down basic materials into the fibers used in making paper
Marbling. Patterns resembling variegated marble; the Persians are credited with its invention
Mold. A wooden frame containing a series of wooden ribs crossed with closely spaced brass wires; the most important tool in papermaking

O **Offset paper.** A paper especially manufactured for use on offset or lithographic presses; also used in letterpress printing

P **Papier-mâché.** Paper pulp mixed with glue and other materials, pressed together, and molded into desired forms or shapes which become hard and strong when dry

Q **Quire.** A set of 25 uniform sheets of paper

R **Ream.** Five hundred sheets of paper
Rice paper. A term applied to paper of a rather coarse character; a misnomer since rice is not generally used in papermaking
Ripple finish. A paper finish sugggestive of ripples produced by an embossing process

S **Signature.** A single printed sheet of paper foled into 8, 12, 16, or more pages
Sizing. Material used to fill the spaces between fibers when manufacturing paper; choice of sizing material depends on the ultimate use of the paper
Substance number. The designation given to sheets of paper in relation to the weight of 500 sheets (one ream) in a standard size

T **Text paper.** The term applied to a grade of paper used for the interior of printed material, such as booklets or advertising printing, as opposed to book paper
Tissue. Very lightweight, transparent paper generally used by artists and designers for preliminary work; heavier weights often used for plans and schematic drawings

V **Vellum.** Calfskin, lambskin, kidskin, etc., treated for use as a writing or printing surface; one of the predecessors of paper, but is not paper
Vellum finish. Paper made with a finish that looks and feels like vellum

W **Watermark.** A translucent insignia, logo, crest, name, or other art or design form visible in paper; produced by the dandy roll in the manufacturing process
Whatman paper. Famous handmade paper, made in England by a process originated by James Whatman, highly prized by contemporary artists
With the grain. Paper folded parallel to the grain

The watermark of Benjamin Franklin

BIBLIOGRAPHY

One of the most important pages in any book may be the Bibliography; the following list of books relating to the subject of paper can serve to help extend your knowledge about various facets relating to this universal material. Because of the interest in papermaking techniques, several books on the subject are also listed.

Heller, Jules. *Papermaking*. New York: Watson-Guptill, 1978. This book defines the various types of paper, including laid, woven, and mold-made and gives step-by-step instructions for making them.

Hunter, Dard. *Papermaking: The History and Techniques of an Ancient Craft*. New York: Dover Publications, 1978. A comprehensive history of the papermaker's craft in every part of the world, this book is liberally illustrated with photographs and diagrams on handmade and machine-made paper.

Johnson, Pauline. *Creating with Paper*. Seattle: University of Washington Press, 1958. Although published some years ago, this is still a valid instructional tool, particularly useful to art teachers. It contains over 200 pages of mostly "how-to-do-it" photographs and diagrams.

Kuo, Nancy. *Chinese Paper Cut Pictures*. London: Alec Tiranti, 1964. This is a charming and sprightly book on Chinese papercutting, with several pages of informative text and many pages of cuttings reproduced in color or on color pages.

Menten, Theodore. *Chinese Cut Paper Designs*. New York: Dover Publications, 1975. This is another book on papercutting. It has only introductory text but almost 90 pages of color and black-and-white illustrations.

Mumford, L. Quincey, Librarian of Congress. *Papermaking*. Washington, D.C.: Library of Congress, 1968. The title page of this handsome and informative book states that it is "an account derived from the exhibition presented in the Library of Congress, Washington, D.C., which opened on April 21, 1968."

Ogami, Hiroshi. *Forms of Paper*. New York: Van Nostrand Reinhold, 1971. This extremely handsome book of beautifully photographed and reproduced forms of paper should be useful for both students and professionals. Diagrams for making some of the illustrated pieces are in the back of the book.

Oka, Hideyuki. *How to Wrap Five Eggs*. New York: Harper & Row, 1967. This is a beautiful and inspirational book that is now out of print but well worth the search for a used copy. It is on traditional Japanese packaging, with many examples in paper as well as in other materials.

Oka, Hideyuki. *How to Wrap Five More Eggs*. New York: John Weatherhill, 1975. Failure to find a copy of the book listed above may be assuaged by the probable availability of this edition, which contains many of the original illustrations found in the first volume, as well as new ones by the same author.

Röttger, Ernst. *Creative Paper Designs*. New York: Van Nostrand Reinhold, 1961. This book on paper designs is primarily for teachers. It has 96 pages of material but no diagrams.

Studley, Vance. *The Art and Craft of Handmade Paper*. New York: Van Nostrand Reinhold, 1977. Precise instructions on ways in which paper can be formed, poured, embedded, layered, and cast are presented together with numerous illustrations.

Tuer, Andrew W. *Japanese Stencil Designs*. New York: Dover Publications, 1967. This reprint of a book originally published c. 1892 has an introductory essay and reproductions of 104 Japanese stencils.

Zeier, Franz. *Paper Construction: Two and Three Dimensional Forms for Artists, Architects and Designers*. New York: Charles Scribner's Sons, 1980. Written and illustrated by a distinguished educator and designer, this book explores the use of paper in experiments between geometry and design. The original German edition, *Papier*, was published in 1974.